AF574408

ECHOES FROM THE HILLS

A DEFINED GUIDE TO COUNTRY SAYINGS

Roland Lee Netzer

First Edition
Volume I
2000

ECHO PUBLISHING SPRINGFIELD MISSOURI

ECHOES FROM THE HILLS

VOLUME I

A Defined Guide To Country Sayings

Roland Lee Netzer

Printed in the United States of America
10 9 8 7 6 5 4 3 2 1

Library of Congress Catalog Card Number
90-80819

ISBN 0-9625768-0-8 Hardcover
ISBN 0-9625768-1-6 Softcover

Technical Consultant Dr. Richard E. Haswell
Book Design Deborah Cartwright
Cover Design Susan Smilanic
Logo Design Jim Osborn
Typist Marjorie Brown Hunt

ECHO PUBLISHING COMPANY
P.O. Box 14482, Springfield, Missouri 65814-0482

ECHOES FROM THE HILLS VOLUME 1

To Katy

The light of my life

ECHOES FROM THE HILLS VOLUME 1

ACKNOWLEDGEMENTS

The nearly 20-year undertaking of writing and defining this collection was not without help from many people. It actually goes back further than that. Some of these sayings are recollections from my childhood in the 1930's as I was raised in a rural community atmosphere where social interaction of verbal nature was an everyday occurrence even though many hours were spent in solitude of agricultural pursuits in the fields. Rural school and church functions like raffles, pie suppers, ice cream socials were all excellent situations where sayings were honed and delivery was practiced to a high degree of excellence. Later in life I traveled extensively and was adept in gleaning those sayings which fit the parameters of being actually accepted back home as part of the vernacular.

To really get the gist of the sayings, personal tones of voice and inflections are sometimes necessary. A later version of this book in audio format will attempt to replicate these sayings, which are characteristically verbal in nature.

Introduction

Welcome to our metaphoric world of words. Here in the beautiful Ozarks mountain region we are fortunate to live in a world ingrained with humorous-to-profound sayings.

These sayings are used in everyday conversation to make a point, invoke laughter or change a line of thought. Some are used as a form of mock threat, usually in handling livestock or pets, but never carried out.

A saying can be used as a form of flattery, hatred, love, amazement, or merely entertainment. The thrust of a saying is what feeling was actually meant to be described. Therefore if a collection of these sayings is to be meaningful, a definition should accompany them. Actually, lexicon or dictionary would be proper terms describing this work.

The real work of this book began in defining a string of words that have been used to create a framework for describing a situation beyond the original definition of each individual word. This soon became a monumental task.

As author, I decided to record the definition of each saying according to my own interpretation. I felt qualified for this challenge after residing for over six decades in primarily rural areas of Missouri.

The original intent of the work was to leave a written record of sayings that were previously largely conveyed only as the spoken word. I thought our grandchildren might get a kick out of reading the old-fashioned, long since discontinued sayings when they are my age.

The collection was started in 1982 with hand written notes in the back of a ledger book being used as a journal. These selections grew into thousands of sayings over the years. Entries were written on scraps of paper carried for such occasions when they came out in casual conversation.

Eventually, each selection, after much evaluation, made it into the innards of a computer for more rapid processing in the evolutionary process which resulted in the pages that follow.

The sorting process consisted of taking out those entries which were commonly used in written form. For instance, sayings, usually verbal in nature, are used in some dictionaries as explanatory material in defining words.

Hill people in general, even though seemingly reticent in nature, are actually outgoing in a comfortable relationship when no strangers are in their midst. This level of comfort leads to creativity and originality of thought when accompanied by a relaxed atmosphere.

Our Ozarkian treasure of metaphoric sayings are not all true native Ozarkian in origin. Natives of rural areas of the Ozarks are generally conservative and patriotic in nature. Upon reaching young adulthood, many followed their forbearers into the military. There they found and brought back to their native land sayings which were then sometimes changed slightly to fit a particular situation.

Returning military personnel were often sought out to tell stories of their travels, experiences and adventures. These stories were embellished with sayings picked up during commingling of cultural influences experienced in the military.

Other sources of supply for country sayings were constant, yet in a state of change, similar to a river that rises and falls in concert with how much rainfall occurs upstream.

Mobility of the rural population contributed to more material for new sayings. In this regard, many natives traveled to distant cities and states for the working part of their lives, only to return to the more pastoral environment of their rural upbringing for retirement.

With them, they brought a colloquial wealth of sayings to be distributed and reused by their peers. Retirees with more time on their hands engaged in activities where casual conversation was a form of entertainment.

Historically, the Ozarks region was blessed with a degree of intellectual freedom from outside influences. This was caused by geographic conditions best described as rather prominent undulations in the earth's surface now known as the Ozark Mountains. From this relative isolation there developed a "do it yourself," "show me" attitude which is prevalent among natives to this day.

As isolation led to home-spun entertainment, humorous sayings were honed to a high degree, resulting in excellent timing and delivery. Humor is broadly splashed through this collection of sayings.

Humor and entertainment go hand in hand in the mountain regions of the Ozarks. During the 60-year period of my use of sayings in the Ozarks, a highly sophisticated entertainment industry developed around the city of Branson, Missouri. Branson is now known as the "live country music entertainment capitol of the world."

In this writer's opinion, a good portion of the success of the entertainment industry in Branson is due to the capacity for giving and receiving humor originating right here in the Ozarks.

As Branson became a tourist entertainment destination point attracting tourists from all over the United States and other parts of the world, the live entertainment shows flourished. Other sources of entertainment entered the Branson arena but the country influence rooted in generations of country sayings is often evident.

As a reading source, this book is sure to become more valuable with time as original verbal expressions from the general population are replaced by professionally written and portrayed audio or video entertainment.

The author makes no claims as to the origin of the sayings published here. I will leave that to more serious research scholars of the written word. I have written down the sayings in order to ensure the primarily spoken colloquialisms do not get lost with time.

To the best of my ability I have recorded the meaning of each of the sayings recorded here according to the most common context in which it was used.

Roland L. Netzer

Springfield, Missouri

January 1, 2000

A

ABOUT AS MUCH FUN AS PETTING A WET CAT
Unpleasant endeavor or encounter.

ABOUT GIVE YOU OUT
Had almost given up on your arrival.

ABOUT RUN TO DEATH
Very busily occupied.
Propane gas delivery men are ... during a severe winter cold spell.

ABOUT TO SEND THE POSSE OUT FOR YOU
Someone arriving late for an appointment is greeted with this statement.

ABOUT TO WOOLLY IT TO DEATH
Playing rough with a pet such as a child dragging a kitten around by the neck.
Also continued concern about a problem or idea.

ABSENCE MAKES THE HEART GROW FONDER
A far away friend becomes more loved as time goes by.

ABSENTMINDED PROFESSOR
A person with the habit of not attending to the more mundane aspects of life.

ABSOLUTE DUMMY
Person or animal behaving unintelligently.

ACCIDENTALLY ON PURPOSE
An act or deed designed to look like a mishap but was deliberately planned.

ACCIDENT LOOKING FOR A PLACE TO HAPPEN
Prone to calamity by neglecting to be cautious.

ACCIDENTS DO HAPPEN

An excuse for a mistake that resulted in an accident.

ACE IN THE HOLE

Any item of value held in reserve for emergency. Refers to stud poker where the face down card is called the "Hole Card".

A CHIGGER THAT'S NO BIGGER THAN THE END OF A PIN, BUT THE BUMP THAT IT RAISES ITCHES LIKE BLAZES; THAT'S WHERE THE RUB COMES IN

Child's rhyme.

ACROSS THE POND

Traversing the Atlantic Ocean from the United States to Europe during WWI.

ACROSS THE TRACKS

Poor section of town.

ACTIONS SPEAK LOUDER THAN WORDS

A project talked about remains just that until the work starts.

ADDING INSULT TO INJURY

Compound degradation.

A DIFFERENCE OF OPINION IS WHAT MAKES HORSE RACES

Let's see who has the best idea by putting them to a test.

A DIFFERENT BREED OF CATS

A change in direction presents an entirely new situation requiring different strategy.

A FARMER TAKES HIS VACATION ONE HALF DAY AT A TIME—WORKS TWELVE HOURS AND OFF TWELVE HOURS

This is a typical example of more truth than jest. Many men and women of the land go for long periods of time working every day without the benefit of a vacation.

AFRAID HE'LL MISS OUT ON SOMETHING

One who stays past time for leaving so as to observe activities of others. Child peeping out of his bedroom after his bedtime and parents are still up and engaged in conversation about the day's activities.

AFRAID OF YOUR SHADOW

Sensitive to possible trouble.
Skittish, timid, shy.

A FRIEND IN NEED IS A FRIEND INDEED

Close companion to the rescue during hard times.

AFTER ALL ELSE FAILS, READ THE DIRECTIONS

Said to a person attempting to assemble a piece of machinery without the aid of instructions.
Laboriously trying to get a machine to work without adequate research as to how to make it work.
"Shade tree mechanics" are good candidates for this advice.

AFTER BIT

In a little while. "Don't worry, they'll be here ...."

AFTER ME YOU COME FIRST

Selfish and covetous with the power to back it up.

AFTER ONE MARTINI—BEST IDEAS I EVER HAD AFTER TWO MARTINIS—SECOND BEST IDEAS AFTER THREE MARTINIS—NO IDEAS AT ALL AFTER FOURTH MARTINI—REFUTE IDEAS SUGGESTED AFTER MARTINI ONE AND TWO

Effects of alcohol on the thought processes are progressively degenerative.

AGAINST THE GRAIN

Contrary to one's instincts or habit. Literally refers to wood.
"That goes ... with me."

A GOOD HEAD OF STEAM UP

Intoxication from drinking alcohol.

AHEAD OF THE GAME
An interim report meaning better progress than the odds would predict.

AIN'T AFRAID OF WORK
A compliment about someone who is industrious.

AIN'T EXACTLY SETTING THE WORLD ON FIRE
Poor performance. Business is slow. Sales way down.

AIN'T GOING TO JOIN THAT FIGHT
Taking no stand on differences of opinion.

AIN'T GOT A LICK OF SENSE
Nincompoop, ninny. Lacking in common sense. Not too bright.

AIN'T GOT NO CHILDREN TO SPEAK OF
Bachelor.

AIN'T GOT THE SENSE GOD GAVE A GOOSE
Not much regard for one's intelligence.

AIN'T LONG FOR THIS WORLD
A very ill person or animal.
Sometimes used humorously about a small illness.

AIN'T MUCH TO LOOK AT
Unattractive.

AIN'T NO BIGGER THAN A THIMBLE
Description of the size of turnips grown in droughty conditions.

AIN'T NOBODY HERE BUT US CHICKENS
Wisecrack remark meaning: I am here alone.

AIN'T NO SKIN OFF MY NOSE
His misfortunes are of no concern to me.

AIN'T SHE A BEAUT?
A good-looking woman or any object.
Attractiveness to perfection.

AIN'T THAT A KICK IN THE SHINS?
Said to a person after an unhappy incident, meaning: That doesn't make you feel very good, does it?

AIN'T THAT ALL-FIRED GOOD LOOKING
Not too impressed with the beauty of another.

AIN'T THAT CUTE?
Derogatory remark indicating dissatisfaction with the antics of another.

AIN'T THAT THE GOD-AWFULLEST MESS YOU EVER SAW?
Things in utter disarray, cluttered, shambles.

AIN'T THAT THE TRUTH
I agree wholeheartedly with what you say.

AIR HAS A LITTLE WHANG IN IT THIS MORNING
First cold snap of the fall.

A LITTLE OF THAT GOES A LONG WAY
Loud noise when you want quiet.
Garlic, hot peppers, or any oppressive irritant.

ALKAFLUENCE OF INKAHOL
Intoxicated. Under the influence of alcohol.

ALL DIRT GOES BEFORE THE BROOM
Unfavorable elements will have to leave when "cleanup time" comes around.

ALL DONE, DING DONG
Job is finished.

ALL DONE UP

Chores finished. Assigned work completed.
Well dressed.

ALL DRESSED UP AND NO PLACE TO GO

A greeting to a visitor who is dressed in his finest.

ALL GOOD THINGS MUST END

Party's over.

ALL IN

Exhausted. Ready for a rest.

ALL OVER BUT THE SHOUTIN'

Project complete.

ALLOWED AS TO HOW

Knew it would happen that way.

ALLOWS TO HOW

I understand his point of view.
I understand his way of doing things.
Will let it happen.
I reckon.
I imagine.

ALL'S WELL THAT ENDS WELL

After trial and tribulation things turn out all right.

ALL THAT JAZZ

You know what I mean, the same old thing.

ALL THE DIFFERENCE IN THE WORLD

Homegrown versus store bought produce. New information changes one's viewpoint.
"As the new baby was being viewed in the nursery, the word was passed that they were secretly married one year ago. That makes ...."

ALL THE GORY DETAILS

Descriptive account of a bad situation.
The facts of the case.
"Skip ..., I have a weak stomach."

ALL THE TEA IN CHINA

Cherished possession with no price tag is wanted by another; and you say, "Wouldn't trade that for ...."

ALL THUMBS

A temporary condition whereby there is a lack of manual dexterity. This is usually used in reference to oneself. I'm ... today.
[It is difficult to type when in this condition.]

ALL WASHED UP

Present condition poor, future bleak.

ALL WE LACK IS FINISHING UP

A job far from complete.

ALMIGHTY DOLLAR

Emphasis on the value of money.
"He has no scruples in the pursuit of ...."

A LOAD OF CHERRIES

A truckload of high quality hogs going to market.

ALREADY YET

Premature event that interrupts what you are doing before it is finished.

ALWAYS KNOCK ON A LADY'S DOOR BEFORE ENTERING

Sign seen on a henhouse door.
Has some merit for the hens will not be frightened as you enter if they hear the rap first.

ALWAYS SINGING THE BLUES

Constant complainer.

A MISS IS AS GOOD AS A MILE

No matter how close the attainment of a goal or objective, failure is the same as if the attempt had never been made.

A MIXED BAG

Proposals or suggestions, some good, some bad.

AN APPLE A DAY KEEPS THE DOCTOR AWAY

Don't overwork your doctor; practice good nutrition.

ANCIENT ENSEMBLE

Old clothing which has come back in style and is in good enough condition to be worn again.

AND ALL THIS TIME YOU THOUGHT I WAS HAVING FUN

Statement by the town drunk to the young beholder of a new hangover.

AND DON'T YOU FORGET IT

Telling someone off and ending the scathing remarks with, "...!"

AND I DON'T MEAN MAYBE

Serious demand. Am absolutely serious.
"Be here at eight o'clock sharp and ...."

AND WHAT HAVE YOU

Used at the end of a descriptive sentence indicating disarray.
The place was filled with junk ....

A NICE PLACE TO VISIT, BUT I WOULDN'T WANT TO LIVE THERE

Any place outside the Ozarks.

ANOTHER COAT OF PAINT AND YOU'D A HAD IT

Escaping a collision with another vehicle by a very narrow margin.

ANOTHER DAY, ANOTHER DOLLAR

Business as usual with a touch of boredom thrown in.

ANOTHER PARTY HEARD FROM
Noise from a different source.
A second person sounding off with the same tune.

ANOTHER STAR IN YOUR CROWN
A person who has just added another admirable act to a long list of others.

ANOTHER THINK A-COMING
The opinion expressed here is that another's ideas are all wrong. If you think I'm crazy enough to go with you to that place you've got ....

ANYBODY HURT IN THAT WRECK?
Said to a person who drives up in a newly purchased automobile.

ANYBODY'S GUESS
Outcome or origin doubtful.
I wonder who the father is? That's ....

ANY JOB WORTH DOING IS WORTH DOING RIGHT
A task undertaken should be given full effort within the limits of capability. Usually said of small or unimportant tasks.

ANY LANDING YOU CAN WALK AWAY FROM IS A GOOD LANDING
Old pilot's saying.

ANYONE WHO WORKS FORTY HOURS A WEEK IN TOWN DOESN'T HAVE TIME TO MAKE ANY MONEY
The sky's the limit if you are self-employed.

ANY PORT IN A STORM
Make do accommodations such as sleeping under a bridge for shelter; any solution to a difficulty.

ANYTHING NOT NAILED DOWN
Watch your possessions.
In some places ... will be stolen if you don't watch it.

ANY WAY YOU SLICE IT
Usually used in the negative.
I cannot accept your argument ....

A PERSON IS KNOWN (JUDGED) BY THE COMPANY HE KEEPS
Your associates of choice reveal your own personality traits.

ARE YOU ALL IN ONE PIECE?
Said to an associate after a harrowing experience.

ARE YOU DECENT?
Called through a closed door before entering to determine whether the occupant is clothed.

ARE YOU EATING A BANANA OR IS THAT YOUR NOSE?
Derogatory remark to one with a large proboscis.
Usually used facetiously by a sibling.

AS BEST YOU CAN
Make do under the circumstances.
I will not be there to help you, so you will have to get by ....

AS EASY AS FALLING OFF A LOG
A simple task for one of experience.

ASK A STUPID QUESTION AND YOU GET A STUPID ANSWER
Example: "Think it will rain?" "Always has."

ASLEEP AT THE SWITCH
Not tending to business.

A SLIP OF THE LIP CAN SINK A SHIP
Words of caution that divulging military information can be dangerous.

AS LUCK WOULD HAVE IT

A mistake is made but everything turns out OK.
Money pouch stolen, but was empty.
Favorable outcome of a precarious situation.

A STEP IN THE RIGHT DIRECTION

Progress, however small, toward a goal.

AS THE WORM TURNS

Certain things will continue no matter what, such as the passage of time.

A STITCH IN TIME SAVES NINE

Repairs done soon prevent serious damage.
Preventative maintenance.

A STONE'S THROW AWAY

A short distance.

AS YE SOW, SO YE SHALL REAP

Seeds of your thoughts or actions may thrive and come back to haunt you.

A TRUSTING SOUL

One who is overly assured of everyone's integrity.

AT THIS STAGE OF THE GAME

Assessment of a project at mid-point.
Somewhere between start and finish.
Too early to tell the outcome.

AT WIT'S END

Puzzled. Don't know where to turn next.

ATTITUDE ADJUSTMENT HOUR

Cocktail party.

AUGHT NINE

Way back when. The year 1909 or 1809 or further back.

A WASH OUT
Any failure.

A WATCHED POT NEVER BOILS
Waiting for the culmination of an activity can be a psychologically time-consuming process.

AW, BALONEY
You are telling me a fib.
An untrue statement gets this response.

AW, DRY UP
Be quiet.

B

BABES IN THE WOODS
Innocence. Ignorant of the facts.

[THE] BABY WASN'T EVEN A GLEAM IN HIS DADDY'S EYE AT THAT TIME
A time in the past more than nine months prior to the birth of a child when the father had not yet become attracted to the mother.

BACK FORTY
A locator phrase meaning the most remote part of the farm.
1/16th of a section of land distant from the farmstead.
As in one taking a long time to come to the phone, the caller says: "I didn't mean to bring you in from the ...."

BACK IN THE COLLAR
Return to work after a vacation. Refers to a workhorse.

BACK TO BACK
As in stud poker and the first up card and the hole card are the same.
Two events in a row.

BACK TO THE BATTLE
Returning to work after a break.

BACK TO THE DRAWING BOARD
Newly designed system, process, or machine breaks down requiring further design modification.

BACK TO THE PITS
Return to work.

BACK UP TO THE PAY WINDOW
Ashamed to draw monetary reward for work of little consequence. "No more work that you do around here, you should ...."

BAD PENNY
Something you are trying to get rid of.
Like a ... it always returns.

BAIL IN OR BAIL OUT
If you are not a part of the solution, then you are a part of the problem. Get with it.

BALD AS AN ONION
Hairless head.

BALDFACED LIE
Blatant fabrication. Lying through his teeth.

BALL AND CHAIN
Derogatory for wife.

BALLED UP
Confused, agitated, prone to make errors in judgment.
Usually preceded by: "All ...."

BALLING THE JACK
Engaged in heavy, strenuous labor. Bowing one's neck.
Accomplishment with speed.

BALL OF FUN

Person who is a joy to be around. Witty, personable.

BARE AS A POOL TABLE

Used sardonically about a neighbor who, due to poor management, lets his cattle graze the pastures too close. "Sparse grazing land ...."

[A] BARGAIN IS NOT A BARGAIN IF YOU DON'T NEED IT

Admonition to those susceptible to sales pitches.

BARKING SPIDERS

Passing gas. Break wind.

BARN DOOR

Rear flap on a suit of one-piece long underwear.
Also refers to the open front fly of a pair of men's trousers or jeans.

BARREL OF A MAN

Male of large build.
Variation: Barrel chested.

BASKETBALL BOTTOM

Large posterior.

BASKET CASE

Severely injured person.

BAT OUT OF GEORGIA

Speeding automobile.
"He came down the road like a ...."

BATS IN THE BELFRY

Lunatic, nutty, idiotic behavior. Crazy acting.

BATTERY ACID

Very strong coffee.

BATTING IT DOWN THE LINE
Fast travel.

BATTING YOUR HEAD AGAINST A BRICK WALL
Futile effort.

BATTLESHIP GRAY
A standard U.S. Navy paint color for ships. Used to denote about any shade of gray.

BEAN FLIPPER
Yoke and handle type slingshot with two rubber launchers attached to a leather missile holding pouch.

BEAN TIME
Noon break for sustenance.

BEAR WITH ME
I shall, after all, correct my mistakes and tread a proper path.

BEAT HIM TO A PULP
Predicted condition of the loser in a fight. "I'm gonna ...."

BEAT HIM UNMERCIFUL
A sound thrashing. Sometimes necessary to load a contrary hog.

BEATS A SNOW BANK
Poor quality livestock feed.
As you feed your livestock less than premium quality hay on a cold winter morn, you tell them, ...

BEAT SEVERELY ABOUT THE HEAD AND SHOULDERS
To pummel. "Warning: I ... for just cause."

BEAT YOU AT YOUR OWN GAME
Using the same tactics as an opponent.

BEAUTY IS IN THE EYE OF THE BEHOLDER
Attractiveness comes in all configurations.

BE CAREFUL, I WANT YOU BACK IN ONE PIECE

Admonition to loved one departing on a journey.

BEDTIME FOR BOZOS

Sleep time for young children.

BEER ON WHISKEY THAT'S PRETTY RISKY WHISKEY ON BEER NOTHING TO FEAR

Admonition by the town drunk.
Refers to the reaction of the stomach to precedence of certain combinations of alcoholic drinks.

BEFORE THE DEW SETS IN

Accomplish tasks early on a summer evening that require the absence of moisture on or near the ground.
"Finish mowing the yard ...."

BEGGARS CAN'T BE CHOOSERS

Accept what you can get without complaint.

[THE] BEGINNING OF THE END

The last battle begins. Pursuing a lost cause.

BE GOOD AND HAVE FUN—BUT IF YOU CAN'T BE GOOD, NAME IT AFTER ME

Admonition to a young woman of the consequences of her actions as she leaves on a date. Usually said by a peer.

BEHAVE YOURSELF

Parting admonition.

BELLY UP

Dead or out of commission as in the case of a dead fish or a capsized ship. Also a bankrupt company.

BENT OUT OF SHAPE

Intoxicated as a result of overindulgence in alcohol.
Sometimes refers to the resulting hangover.

BENT OVER BACKWARDS

Extra effort.
"I ... for him and what did I get—a slap in the face."

BE ON THE SAFE SIDE

Take precautions.

BET YOU ANY AMOUNT OF MONEY

Sure as sure can be that I am right.

BE THERE, BABY

Pleading emotionally for yet unknown results to turn out positive.
Such as drawing a card from the deck to fill out a hand.
[While arrowhead hunting and seeing just the tip of a point sticking out of the ground and hoping it was a complete unbroken artifact I would say, "...."]

BE THERE FOREVER

A project so time consuming that it becomes counterproductive.

BETTER DEAD THAN RED

Death is preferable to communist domination.

BETTER SAFE THAN SORRY

Cautious approach pays off in the long run.

BETTING ON THE COME

A chancy situation where the success or failure is not known until some time in the future. Undertake a venture involving risk capital.

BEWARE OF ANYONE WHO PRONOUNCES THE WORD DOLLAR "DOLLAH"

The sign of a fast pitch salesman.

BIBLE THUMPER

Overzealous pastor or member of the congregation.

BIG BRUISER

A large man in good fighting trim.

BIG BUCKS

A lot of money.
"He moved to California where they make those ...."

BIG CABIN IN THE SKY

Heaven.

BIG DEAL

So what?

BIG END OF IT

Task or amount almost complete.
I use this term when a customer's bill comes to $5.10, he hands me a $5.00 bill, and while he digs in his pocket for the dime, I say: "That's the ...."

BIGGEST DUCK ON THE PUDDLE

Best or leader of a small group, usually one who failed in a large group.

BIG OLD GOODUNS OR GOOD OLD BIGUNS

Word gymnastics used as a time filler and attempt at humor.
"Our watermelons are all large and of excellent quality, so which do you want, ...?"

BIN-BUSTER

A large crop of corn or other grain.

BIRDS OF A FEATHER FLOCK TOGETHER

Groupings by common interests.
Usually applied to a group of bad mannered persons.

BITING THE HAND THAT FEEDS YOU

Opposing a benefactor. The phrase is critical of the biter.

BIT OFF MORE THAN HE CAN CHEW

Excessive ambition.
Taking on more projects than capabilities merit.

BLACK AS THE ACE OF SPADES
Used to describe the color of an animal.

BLANK AS A TOAD
Expression of ignorance on one's face.
Complete lapse of memory leaves this look on one's face.

BLEEDING LIKE A STUCK HOG
An injury compared to the butchering of swine.
Stuck in this case refers to the incision made to induce drainage of blood from the tissue.

BLESS YOUR HEART
Thank you kindly.

BLIND AS A BAT
Animal who can't find its stall.
Some umpires and referees are said to be ....

BLIND IN ONE EYE AND CAN'T SEE OUT OF THE OTHER
A horse with good eyesight but needs constant reining to follow a row.
A person indifferent to the facts.

BLISTER STAGE
Immature sweet corn.

BLOODY SHAME
Bloody Mary without the vodka.

BLOW AND GO
Proceeding at full steam. Maximum output.

BLOW HIM TO KINGDOM COME
To shoot and kill. Usually used with reference to killing a varmint in the henhouse. Kingdom come is heaven.

BLOW YOU SKY HIGH
In dealing with explosives of any sort this can be the result if caution is not used. (Blow in this case meaning "leave.")

BOBBSEY TWINS

Inseparable pair, referring to a children's book series of the 1940's.

BODY EXCHANGE

A place where people meet to pair off.
Singles bar.

BOILING MAD

Furious to the point of fighting.

BOLT FROM THE BLUE

Sudden appearance. New idea. Literally lightning in a clear sky.

BONE COLD

Chilled through from being exposed to inclement weather with inadequate clothing.

BOODLE UP A STORM

Making mad passionate love.
Heavy petting.

BORED OF EDUCATION

High school doodling on notebook and graffiti on walls.
The pun is on Board.

BORING HOLES IN THE SKY

Aircraft in flight. Used by pilots in training with no particular destination in mind.

BORING WITH A BIG AUGER

Operating on a large scale.

BORN LOSER

A person with a long record of failures.
Ne'er-do-well.

BORROW FIRE

Go to a neighbor for live coals as you have let your fire go out. "Charlie, you will have to go next door and ... as the

embers have expired overnight."
Generally, get help.

BOTTOMLESS PIT
Heavy eater.
Most teenage boys seem to be a ....

BOUGHT THE FARM
Serviceman killed in action and his life insurance policy pays off the mortgage on his parents' farm.

BOUGHT YOUR BOOKS AND SENT YOU TO SCHOOL
Still didn't learn anything.

[A] BOUNCING BABY BOY
New born male child.

BOUNCING ON THE PEG
Fuel tank gauge showing almost empty.

BOWL CUT
A type of haircut whereby the result is similar to bangs all the way around the head. As if a bowl had been inverted on the head and all hair extending past the edge (rim) is clipped off.

BOW YOUR NECK
Intense determination.

BOX YOUR JAWS
Threat of a swat to the face.
Slap in the kisser.
Usually said to children as a false threat. "I'll ... if you don't stay out of the cookie jar."

BOY, DID THEY EVER
Exceeding expectation.

BOY, HOWDY
Exclamation of agreement with another's statement.

[A] BOY IN MAN'S CLOTHES
A boy or young adult forced into responsibilities of an older person.

BOYS WILL BE BOYS
Doting mother's remark at the not-so-nice actions of her sons.

BOY, YOU GOT IT ROUGH
Sarcastic way of saying some have all the luck.
While you slave away on a hot summer day, a kitten sleeps in the shade nearby and gets this comment from you, ...

BRAGGED TOO SOON
Unforeseen events change the picture.

BRAGGING OR COMPLAINING?
In answer to a statement of dual meaning.
"I got sick yesterday and couldn't go to work." "...."
(Likes being off from work but not being sick.)
"My car will go 100 miles per hour." "...."
(Are you saying that is good, or do you think it should go faster?)

BRAINLESS WONDER
Devoid of common sense but is in a leadership position.
Inept military officers are sometimes called ...s.

BRAND, SPANKING NEW
Fresh out of the factory and never used before.

BRAVE SOUL
One who ventures into dangerous circumstances over a trifling matter.
A few ...s ventured out to our farm to buy eggs during the snow storm.

BREAK OUT IN A NEW PLACE
As you try to get a word in edgewise the other person changes the subject and continues to dominate the conversation.

After a series of troubles, chaos continues from another direction. When you correct one weak spot, another will develop.

BREAKS ME UP

Spontaneous laughter results when I hear a joke.

BREAK YOU

Excessive spending will ....

BRIGHT-EYED AND BUSHY-TAILED

Early riser ready for action.

BRING ON THE DANCING GIRLS

Let the party begin.

BROKEN RECORD

Verbally and excessively repetitive. Repeating one's views to the point of being obnoxious.

BROWN AS AN INDIAN

Very suntanned.

BUCKET OF BOLTS

Old decrepit vehicle.

BUG OUT

Keep your nose out of my business, you busybody.

BUILDING MONUMENTS TO OURSELVES

Unneeded project undertaken just to show off one's ability.

BUILT-IN FAMILY

A woman marrying a man who already has children, or vice versa.

BULGING AT THE SEAMS

Full bag—anything over-full.

BULLET WITH YOUR NAME ON IT WASN'T THERE

Combat survivor.

BURNING UP THE HIGHWAY

Driving fast.

A neighbor making many trips to town in one day.

BURN OUT

Acceleration rate of an automobile so rapid that the driving wheels spin on the surface.

Also used as a way of saying "Hurry up, let's get moving."

One who has worked so long he can't face a new job.

BURNT UP WITH GREASE

As you replace a bearing that became defective due to the lack of lubrication, a friend remarks sarcastically: "That old bearing looks to me like it was ...."

BURR UNDER YOUR SADDLE

Facetiously indicating your displeasure with the irritability of another.

Literally, it is a continuing irritation to the horse.

When someone is irritable you say: "You got a ...?"

BUSIER THAN A BIRD DOG

Fervent activity. Actively engaged in pursuit of a job.

BUSTING A GUT

Overdoing it. Excessive effort applied to a job or project.

BUST YOUR BUTTONS

Great pride. Extra effort applied to get the job done.

BUSY AS A BEE

Working rapidly.

BUSY AS A CRANBERRY MERCHANT

Intensely occupied.

BUTCHER BILL

Nickname for a small town barber known for his white sidewall haircuts.

BUTTER AND EGG MAN FROM THE WEST (EAST, SOUTH, NORTH)

A greeting to a delivery person as he arrives, no matter what the cargo being carried.
"Here comes the ..., give him room."

BUTTER HATCHETS

A child's first teeth.

BUTTON HEAD

One of limited intelligence in your opinion.

BUTTON YOUR LIP

Don't say a word about this.

BUYING OUT THE WHOLE PLACE

Refers to a customer who is making an extremely large purchase.

BUYS AT RETAIL
SELLS AT WHOLESALE
AND PAYS THE FREIGHT BOTH WAYS

A farmer's method of operation.

BUZZARD BAIT

Decrepit. Usually refers to an old horse.

BY GOSH AND BY GORY

"Well glory be."

BY GUESS AND BY GOSH

Getting there in a haphazard way. A chancy situation. Flying an aircraft without navigational aids.

C

CACKLE BERRIES

The reproductive package of the domesticated fowl.
In other words, chicken eggs.
Variation: hen apples.

CALIFORNIA SUNSHINE

Rain, in Missouri.

CALLED HIS HAND

The bluff is challenged.
Refers to action in poker, ending play and requiring show of cards.

CALM, COOL, AND COLLECTED

Unshakable under fire.
The opposite of all shook up.

CAME OUT OF IT SMELLING LIKE A ROSE

Results much better than expected.

CAN DO

Positive attitude.

CAN DO NO WRONG

A trusted friend whose judgement you feel is superior.
Sometimes used in a derogatory sense as in the case of a doting parent who feels his child ....

CAN HEAR A MOUSE WALKING ON COTTON

Acute auditory capability.
"You think he's deaf? Why, he ...."

CAN READ A NEWSPAPER THROUGH IT

Thin piece of meat on a sandwich.

CAN'T BEAT THAT WITH A STICK

A very good deal.

CAN'T CARRY A TUNE IN A BUCKET
Musical ability limited.

CAN'T GET BLOOD OUT OF A TURNIP
Inability to collect a debt because of a lack of funds on the part of the debtor.

CAN'T HEAR MYSELF THINK
Distracting noise disrupts mental concentration.

CAN'T HIT THE BROAD SIDE OF A BARN
Poor shot.

CAN'T KEEP A GOOD MAN DOWN
Resiliency under stress. Bouncing back after adversity.

CAN'T LIVE WITH THEM AND CAN'T LIVE WITHOUT THEM
Spouses after many years of marriage.

CAN'T MAKE A SILK PURSE OUT OF A SOW'S EAR
Social climber who cannot change old ways. The nouveau riche often carry old ways to their new environment.

CAN'T PLEASE THEM ALL
In retail sales some people cannot be accommodated.

CAN'T PROVE IT BY ME
I am ignorant of the facts with regard to the subject you have broached.

CAN'T PUT MY FINGER ON IT
Elusive suspicion.

CAN'T SAY AS I DO
I disagree with your question.
"Do you think the president is doing a good job? "...."

CAN'T SEE THE FOREST FOR THE TREES
Big picture clouded by too much attention to details.

CAN'T TEACH AN OLD DOG NEW TRICKS

Difficult to change an established way of doing things.

CAN'T WIN THEM ALL

A temporary setback.
An adventure turns into a disaster.

CAN'T WIN FOR LOSING

After a series of misfortunes, a feeling of futility follows.

CARDS ARE STACKED IN THEIR FAVOR

Group or individual who, due to the laws of the land, has the advantage.
Stacking cards is pre-arranging them to guarantee winning.

CARRIED AWAY

Engrossed in a project to the point of being ridiculous.
Overzealous.

CAST IRON STOMACH

A person who has the belly of a billy goat.
Consumes food of such quantity and quality that it would make an ordinary person sick.

CATCH A FELLA

Used by an unmarried female looking for a spouse.
Girl with inclination toward marriage is out to ....

CATCH YOU ON THE FLIP FLOP

Truckers' citizens band radio lingo meaning: I will talk to you again as we return from our respective trips and cross paths again. The older phrase was, "Catch you on the rebound."

CAT GOT YOUR TONGUE?

Trying to elicit verbal response from a reticent child to no avail.

CAT'S MEOW

Dressed in the newest fashion. Flamboyant. A person who is overdressed for the occasion.

Persons with a higher regard for themselves than is justified. "They thought they were the ...."

CAUGHT BETWEEN A ROCK AND A HARD PLACE
A position where movement in any direction is likely to bring adverse results.

CAUGHT IN A WEB
Entangled; ... of your own making.

CBM FARMERS (CORN, BEANS AND MIAMI)
Wealthy farmers of the midwest who, after the harvest of their corn and beans (soybeans) in the fall, go to Miami, Florida, for the winter. Very few of these left (1985).

CHALK THAT UP TO EXPERIENCE
Learn from your mistakes.

CHEAPO REPO
A car, or any merchandise, taken back because of failure to make payments.

CHEER UP; THINGS COULD BE WORSE. SO I CHEERED UP AND SURE ENOUGH THINGS GOT WORSE
A defeatist attitude with pun intended.

CHEESE BAG
A person who dresses in cheap or inappropriate clothing. One who acts or dresses in a manner contrary to your principles.

[THE] CHEESE THAT BINDS
Uncomfortable situation. Sticky situation.

CHEWING IT UP AND SPITTING IT OUT
A combine threshing machine moving smoothly and expeditiously through a heavy field of grain. Can be used for other machines that are operating at capacity.

CHICKENS COME HOME TO ROOST
Your past misdeeds will haunt you.

CHIEF COOK AND BOTTLE WASHER
Husband who takes over the kitchen chores while the wife is away.

CHILDREN SHOULD BE SEEN AND NOT HEARD
Admonition to noisy youngsters.

CHILI TODAY AND HOT TAMALE
Facetious statement of weather now and to come.

CHOMPING AT THE BIT
Impatient with delay in getting project under way.

CHROME DOME
Bald headed.

CITY COUSINS
Metropolitan relatives of a rural resident.

CLAIM TO FAME
"Why does he think he is so important? What's his ...?"

CLEAN AS A HOUND'S TOOTH
Very shiny, immaculate.

CLEAN HIS PLOW
Threat of retribution for past, present or future misdeeds. "If he continues to pester my sister I'll ...."

CLEANLINESS IS NEXT TO GODLINESS
Body and soul in tune.

CLEAN LIVING KID
A person who gives up a series of bad habits in preference of a more wholesome life.

CLEAN SWEEP
All enemy ships sunk; winning everything.

CLEAR AS A BELL
Azure skies.

CLEARED OUT
Departed the area.
"I haven't seen a coyote in a quite a spell. They must have ...."

CLEVER, THOSE CHINESE
Innovative device regardless of the designer. Said while viewing a cute contrivance.

CLIMBING THE WALLS
Cabin fever. Mock hysteria. Stir crazy.
After a long period of confinement due to bad weather, a feeling of panic or anxiety ensues.

CLINGING VINE
Adoration of a man by a woman to the point of being overly dependent.
A woman totally enmeshed in her mate's dominance.

CLOSE THE BARN DOOR AFTER THE HORSE IS STOLEN
Well intentioned actions—ill timed.

CLOSE THE DOOR—YOU'RE LETTING THE FLIES OUT
Reverse psychology intended to attract the attention of children to the plight of the mother who is trying to keep the living spaces sanitary and insect free.

[THE] COAST IS CLEAR
Nothing coming this way, go ahead.

COB IT
Rapid acceleration by an automobile.

COBWEB BAR—SPIDER SPEAKING
Smart-alecky way to answer the phone.

COCKED AND PRIMED

Ready for action.
Ready to go.
Ready to roll.

COFFEE HOUND

One who drinks coffee to excess.

COLD HANDS, WARM HEART DIRTY FEET, NO SWEETHEART

Coolness at the extremities has no bearing on true feeling. Said during a handshake or hand holding in cool weather by the one with the warmest hands.

COLD HARD CASH

Payment in currency or coin rather than by check.

COLD STONE SOBER

Not inebriated.

COME A GOOD'UN

Description of heavy precipitation.
After the fact, it's "came a good'un."
Also used futuristically as in: "The way it's snowing it could ... by morning."

COME-ALONG

A hand winch with ratchet and cable for moving heavy objects horizontally or vertically.

COME AND GET IT

Call to dinner.

COME IN, LOOK OUT, YOU CAN SEE FARTHER

A greeting at your front door to a welcome visitor.

COME ON OVER AND WE'LL OPEN A KEG OF NAILS

Inviting someone over for a drink and a visit.

COMES AND GOES

State of the mind with regard to lucidity; usually refers to old people.

COMES BY IT NATURALLY

Like father like son.
Inherited traits.

COME-SIT A SPELL

Invitation to a good friend to stay and visit for awhile.

COME TO FIND OUT

Revelation after a long period of ignorance.

COME TO THINK OF IT

Thought-provoking activity brings forth a long forgotten bit of information.

COMING AROUND

Regaining consciousness.

COMING ON STRONG

Persistent, amorous suitor.
Abundant production as in hens laying well or vegetable plants producing a good crop.

COMING OUT OF THE KINKS

Resurgence.
Following a long dry spell the crops rebound after a slow steady rain.

COMING RIGHT ON DOWN

A hard rain.

COMMENCING TO BEGIN

Getting ready to start on a project.

COMMON AS YOUR OLD SHOE

A wealthy or prominent person who retains humble ways.

CONSPICUOUS BY HIS ABSENCE
A person who should be in a certain place but is not. "Since the groom didn't show up for the wedding, he is ...."

CONTRIBUTING TO THE CAUSE
Helping out.

COOKIE DUSTER
Mustache.

COOKING ON THE FRONT BURNER
Project progressing with optimum speed and enthusiasm.

COOKING UP A STORM
Preparing an elaborate meal.
Any busy, complicated and elaborate activity.

COOL AS A CUCUMBER
Steady under fire. Performance not altered by pressure. The ability to maintain presence of mind in the face of adversity. Bullets were flying everywhere and there he stood ....

COOL CAT
A dapper male with composure.

COOL DOWN, PAPA; YOU'RE GONNA BLOW YOUR TOP
Statement to overly sexually stimulated partner.

COOLER HEADS PREVAILED
A dangerous situation averted by the presence of persons with a common sense approach to the situation.

COOLLY SAP
One who keeps cool under duress.
Calm, cool and collected.

CORRECT ME IF I'M WRONG
What I am about to say you may know more about than I do.

COULD GO TO CUMULATING

Snow fall getting heavier with big flakes.

COULDN'T GET THEM ALL IN A FORTY-ACRE FIELD

Many relatives at family reunion.

COULDN'T HAVE HAPPENED TO A BETTER FELLOW

Something good happened to a deserving friend.

COULDN'T MAKE HEADS NOR TAILS OUT OF IT

Indecipherable or incomprehensible.

COUNTRY COUSINS

Rural relatives of metropolitan residents.

COW PASTURE POOL

Golf.

COXIES (COX'S) ARMY

A shabby bunch of disreputable persons. Motley crew.
Sometimes refers to a large family traveling together.
"When they all get together and go to town it looks like ...."

CRACKER BOX

A new home built out of shoddy materials.

CRACK ON THE COCO

Swat to the head.
"Mind your manners or I'll give you a ...."

CRAP CALLS

Craps is a game of chance using two cubes (dice) with spots of 1 to 6 on each cube.
Two, three and twelve are losing first rolls in dice.
Seven and eleven are winning first rolls of dice.
Four, five, six, eight, nine and ten are called for fervently on each throw after the first roll to bring about a repeat and a win.
2 Snake eyes.

3 Trey.
4 Little Joe from Kokomo.
5 Fever in the south and I'm the doctor.
6 Route Sixty Six.
7 Seven come eleven baby needs new shoes.*
8 Eight-skate and donate.
9 Nina Brown.
10 Big Dick.
11 Seven come eleven baby needs new shoes.*
12 Box cars.
* This call is always made as you make the first roll of the dice.

CRAZIER THAN A PET COON
Facetiously telling someone he is acting in an unorthodox manner.

CREEP AND RECREEP
Two associates whose motives and behavior you question.

CRIED THE SALE
The auctioneer who officiates at a public auction.
"Who ... for you?"

CROOKED AS A BARREL OF SNAKES
Used to describe such things as a winding pathway, switchback road, row of corn or windrow of hay.
Sometimes used to denote a person who leans toward the unethical in financial affairs.

CROSS THAT BRIDGE WHEN I GET TO IT
Deferred decision.
Undeniable event requiring a decision in the future but not enough information at hand to form a plan of action.
"What are you going to do about the note that is due next week?" "I'll ...."

CRUMB BUM
Beggar who will take anything.
Indolent ne'er-do-well.

CRYING THE BLUES
Always complaining.

CRY ON MY SHOULDER
I will share your grief with you.

CURBSTONE CUTIE
Female wishing to be picked up.

CURIOSITY KILLED THE CAT
Being too nosy can get you in trouble.
Poke your nose into other people's business at your own risk. A way of saying, "Stay out of my affairs," or " Do not ask me to divulge a secret."
Variation: ... but a cat has nine lives.

CUSSING THE DRIVER
Squeaking wheel on a farm wagon needing lubrication.

CUTE AS A BUG'S EAR
A person or object with adorable characteristics.

CUT HIM DOWN TO SIZE
Intentional demoralizing remark made to a pompous person.

CUTTING HIS TEETH
New man on the job.

CUT YOUR FOOT
Barnyard lingo.
You step in fresh animal feces and a friend asks ...?

CUT YOUR WATER OFF
Discontinue supply goods or services.
Usually the result of exceeding the credit limit.

D

DANG NIGH
Almost.

DARK 30
After twilight.

DAY LATE AND A DOLLAR SHORT
Missed another opportunity by being tardy.
Always behind and short of funds.

DEAD SERIOUS
Most certainly not joking.
Means business to the extreme.

DEAD TO THE WORLD
Asleep.

DEAF AS A POST
Indifferent to frequent verbal requests.

DEEP TROUBLE
A state of severe distress.
Excuses only exacerbate the problem for one who is in ....

DEN OF INIQUITY
A bad place.
Low class bar.
Where undesirables hang out.

DER LOUDENBOOMER WITH A BIG KEBANG
Atomic bomb.

DESCENDED LIKE THE PLAGUE
A sudden overall calamity.
A severe scolding.

DETERMINED LITTLE CUSS

Child makes a goal of being top in the class and does it. Extremely motivated.

DEVIL DOG

A small whirlwind.
Dust devil.

DID IT UP BROWN

A job done either real good or real bad.

DIDN'T BAT AN EYE

An expected reaction not forthcoming.
"I shot him a price and he ...; just whipped out his checkbook and paid me."

DIDN'T GIVE IT A FAIR TEST

As in judging a crop variety that was subjected to adverse growing conditions making comparison difficult.

DIDN'T KNOW HE HAD IT IN HIM

Astounding performance by a presumed incompetent.

DIDN'T PUT A DENT IN IT

Little progress.
"She prepared so much food that we ...."

DIDN'T REGISTER

I heard but did not understand.

DIDN'T SAY THANK YOU, KISS MY FOOT, OR NOTHING

Good deed brings no praise.

DIDN'T TAKE TOO KINDLY TO THAT

Took offense.
"When I took his girl friend away from him he ...."

DIDN'T TURN A TAP

No work done.

DID THE TRICK

Tipped the scales in your favor.
After repeated effort a slight change in strategy brings success.

DID WE EVER

Verification.
"Did you have much snow at your house last night?" "...."

DID YOU DROP THE SET OUT OF YOUR RING?

Statement after hearing a loud noise from a heavy falling object hitting the floor.

[THE] DIE IS CAST

Irrevocable forces put in motion. The stage is set.
Preliminary acts have been done, now we wait for the results.
Two interpretations here: Die is one dice. You've rolled and it's out of your control. Also, a die has been cast in the mold, its form is set for good.

DIFFERENT AS NIGHT FROM DAY

Opposite of two peas in a pod.

DIFFERENT STROKES FOR DIFFERENT FOLKS

To each his own.

DIFFERENT TURNED

One who has traits different from those of siblings.

DING DONG DADDY FROM DUMAS AND YOU OUGHTA SEE ME DO MY STUFF

Used during the 1940s by young males in a boastful vein.
Usually refers to sexual encounters. "I'm a ...."

DIRTY BERT

Underhanded person.

DIVE IN SHALLOW

Proceed with caution.
Your answer to a person who has just explained his plans for

an elaborate, extensive project requiring much money, time, and effort.

DO AS I SAY, NOT AS I DO

I am far from perfect and I want you to be better than I.
"Daddy, you say 'ain't'!" "You ...."

DO DIDDLY SQUAT

Nothing accomplished. Very little. Description of a person who acts as if he has means but in reality does not.
"He hasn't got ...."

DOESN'T CARE WHETHER SCHOOL KEEPS OR NOT

Indifferent. Lack of concern.

DOESN'T EAT ENOUGH TO KEEP A BIRD ALIVE

Fastidious feeder.
A person with little regard for gustatory delights.
Usually refers to an elderly person with a poor appetite due to inactivity.
Variation: Eats like a bird.

DOESN'T HAVE A LEG TO STAND ON

Poor bargaining position.
Weak case.

DOESN'T MISS A TRICK

A very observant person.

DOG AND PONY SHOW

Traveling salesman promoting a scheme intended to separate you from your money to his advantage.

DOG HAIR

Very fine wiry grass difficult to cut with a mowing machine.

DO IT, THEN TALK ABOUT IT

Advice to one who sometimes brags too soon.

DO IT TO IT

Accelerate rapidly. Give the car the gas and let's get moving.

DONE ALL THE DAMAGE WE CAN DO HERE

Job completed and moving on to the next work site.

DO NOT THROW CIGARETTE BUTTS IN THE URINAL; IT MAKES THEM SOGGY AND HARD TO LIGHT

Graffiti on the washroom wall. Written by someone who picks up cigarette butts for reuse.

DON'T BELIEVE ANYTHING YOU HEAR AND HALF WHAT YOU SEE

Things are not always as they seem.
Beware of the validity of gossip.
Skeptical.

DON'T BELIEVE I'LL FOOL WITH IT

Not interested in your proposition.

DON'T CHANGE HORSES IN THE MIDDLE OF THE STREAM

Last minute deviation from a planned course of action should be given careful thought.

DON'T CONDEMN THE APPLE IF YOU ARE THE TREE

Hesitate before being critical of your children for they are generally copying or mirroring your own traits.

DON'T COUNT YOUR CHICKENS BEFORE THEY HATCH

Unforeseen events may alter outcome of a venture.

DON'T CRY OVER SOMETHING THAT CAN'T CRY OVER YOU

Material possessions can be replaced in the event of loss and should not cause undue alarm. On the other hand, loved ones are irreplaceable. Used in reference to a home burning down and no one injured.

DON'T DO ANYTHING I WOULDN'T DO (First Person); THAT GIVES ME LOTS OF ROOM (Second Person)
Said to someone leaving on a date or a trip.

DON'T EVER CARRY ANY MORE MONEY ON YOU THAN YOU CAN AFFORD TO LOSE
Beware of the possibility of losing your money at all times.

DON'T EVER BRAG ON YOUR DOGS OR YOUR KIDS, THEY WILL ALWAYS LET YOU DOWN
Offspring or canine praise should be kept to yourself if you wish to avoid embarrassment. They exhibit an inevitable lack of success when bragged upon. In the hills, a hunting dog's abilities are held in almost as high esteem as those of a son or daughter.

DON'T FIX IT IF IT AIN'T BROKE
Premature repair or adjustment of a machine can be counterproductive. Tinkering with a machine that is still doing its job sometimes results in getting it out of adjustment and rendering it inoperative.
Variation: If it ain't broke, don't fix it.

DON'T GET EXCITED ABOUT THE MOON LIGHT THAT REFLECTS UPON A LOG
Calm down, there is nothing to worry about, I will protect and take care of you in the event of a calamity. You are worrying for naught.
Talking to your horse while riding cross country on a moonlit night you say ....

DON'T GET TOO THICK WITH THEM, THEY WILL RUN YOUR DOORS IN
Admonition that an obtuse group will take advantage of your hospitality if you are not careful.
"A new family moved in down the road but ...."

DON'T GIVE A DAMN PILLS
Tranquilizers.

DON'T GIVE ME THAT
Quit teasing me.

DON'T GIVE UP TILL THEY PUT THE LAST SHOVEL FULL ON YOU
Fending off the grim reaper with a positive attitude.

DON'T GO ANY PLACE YOU WOULDN'T TAKE YOUR MOTHER
Navy chaplain's admonition before departing on liberty at a port of call. This works pretty well unless your mother is a prostitute.

DON'T HAVE ANYTHING BETTER TO DO
Idle person engaged in idle pursuits.

DON'T HAVE THE FOGGIEST
I have no idea.

DON'T HOLD YOUR BREATH
Something not apt to happen soon.

DON'T JUST STAND THERE—DO SOMETHING—EVEN IF IT'S WRONG
Inaction in the face of calamity often nets poor results.
Variation: "Do something—lead, follow, or get out of the way."

DON'T KNOW WHICH END IS UP
Confused.

DON'T KNOW WHICH SIDE THEIR BREAD IS BUTTERED ON
Describing those who ignore the source of the bounty.

DON'T KNOW WHICH WAY TO TURN
Confusion due to lack of direction.
A state of mind after a calamitous occurrence.

DON'T LEAVE IT FOR AN INSTANT
Your undivided guardianship is required constantly.

DON'T LET IT GET YOU DOWN
Stay cool under duress.

DON'T LET THE CAT OUT OF THE BAG
I have entrusted you with this secret, so defer the temptation to reveal it.

DON'T LET YOUR DREAMS GROW OLD WITH YOU
Put your secret reveries into action while you are physically and mentally capable of carrying them to successful completion.

DON'T LOOK AT ME
I am innocent. I am not responsible for, nor guilty of that act. Reaction to a withering stare.

DON'T MAKE A BIG PRODUCTION OUT OF IT
Stop telling gossip far and wide. Too much ado about nothing.
Be charitable when someone errs and let it go at that.

DON'T PICK UP ANY WOODEN NICKELS
Parting statement to a person going on a trip.
Simply means: be careful in your dealings as you travel far from home.
Variation: "Don't take any wooden nickels."

DON'T PUT ALL YOUR EGGS IN ONE BASKET
You can profit by diversification.
Variation: Put all your eggs in one basket—then watch the basket. Means the opposite—specialize.

DON'T RIGHTLY KNOW
Not sure enough of the facts to answer your question.
"How far do you think it is to the moon?" "...."

DON'T RUSH OFF IN THE HEAT OF THE DAY
Used year around. In winter facetiously.
Please stay awhile longer, I like your company.
Answer is: "I won't. I'll go real slow."

DON'T SELL YOURSELF SHORT
Keep confidence in your abilities.
Toot your own horn.

DON'T SEND A BOY TO DO A MAN'S JOB
Degradation of incompetent adult male worker who has failed at a task.

DON'T SPEND IT ALL IN ONE PLACE
Admonition when someone is given a pittance.
"Here's a quarter, ..."

DON'T STICK BEANS IN YOUR NOSES
Admonition to children by parents when leaving them alone at home for a short while.
Otherwise don't do anything foolish.

DON'T STRAIN YOUR MILK
Caution against overexertion in lifting a heavy object.

DON'T THAT BEAT A HEN A-PECKING
Amazement.
A new innovative device is reacted to verbally by saying, ...

DON'T THAT BEAT ALL
Amazement.
Comment by Curtice Williams, Sr., when he and a friend encountered the local storekeeper inebriated at his place of business.

DON'T THAT KNOCK YOUR HAT IN THE CREEK
Surprised at the actions of another. Reaction to unexpected event.

DON'T THINK THEY WON'T
Never underestimate the resolve of your adversaries.

DON'T WE ALL

Universally acceptable conditions.

As the sun comes out on a cold winter day and warms everything it touches, one comments: "I sure do like the sunshine."

The response is: "...."

DON'T WORRY YOUR PRETTY LITTLE HEAD

I'll take care of my own problems without your help or concern. Answer to concern that is obviously fake.

DO OR DIE

A call for extreme effort in the performance of a task.

DOOR SLAMMERS

Facetious name for small children.

Variations: Rug Rats, Ankle Biters, Cookie Snatchers.

DOUBLE SHOVEL

A one-horse cultivator with two staggered plow points about five inches wide and twelve inches apart. Cultivates deeper than a scratcher. When used on tall corn it will throw soil up around the stems in order to smother out small weeds in the row with the corn.

DOWN BOY

A female rejection to the amorous advances of a male.

DOWN IN THE HUNKERS

Stiff legs.

DOWN THE HATCH

Drinking toast.

DOWN THE TUBES

Failurc.

DOWN TO NOTHING

Financial reverses create substantial poverty.

DOWN TO THE WIRE

Avoiding a decision until the last minute. Outcome doubtful due to unknown factors lurking in the shadows. Refers to the finish line in horse racing.

DOWN YOUR SUNDAY THROAT

Food in the windpipe.

DRANK ENOUGH TO FLOAT A BATTLESHIP

Description of the town drunk.

DRAW BACK A BLOODY STUB

Warning that if you take a swat at me, you will suffer this consequence.
"Go ahead, take a poke at me and you'll ...."

DRAW THEIR BREATH AND THEIR PAY

Persons engaged in work which is of little importance.
Monetary reward for doing nothing.

DROOPY DRAWERS

A young child.

DROPPED A BUNDLE

Lost a lot of money such as at the horse races.

DROPPED HIM LIKE A HOT POTATO

Spurned lover.
When it was discovered he was cheating on her, she ....

DROPPING LIKE FLIES

Casualties in large numbers.
Rapid death in large numbers in a flock of chickens due to an acute illness.

DROWNED RATS

Appearance of children after a swimming party.
"You look like ...."

DROWN HIS SORROWS

Solve problems with alcohol.

DROWNING YOU OUT

A loud noise such as a radio which masks the words of another.

DRUNK AS A HOOT OWL

Intoxicated from over indulgence in alcohol. Tight. Inebriated.

DRY AS A TINDERBOX

Extreme lack of moisture.

DRY SPOT IN MY GUZZLE TOOT

Scratchy throat.

DUCK'S NEST

A comparatively small pond with a water surface area of less than one-fourth acre.

DUKE'S MIXTURE

Any combination of various species or varieties.
A combination of several tobaccos to obtain the desired flavor and aroma.
Potpourri. Conglomeration.

DUMB JERK

Uninformed, ignorant, uneducated, stupid. A blunder brings this retort.
"You ...!" Observation of an associate after a particularly stupid move.

DUMB LIKE A FOX

Actions appear to be stupid but are a planned ploy devised to divert attention.

E

EAGLE EYE FLEEGLE
Very observant.

EARLY TO BED, EARLY TO RISE, MAKES A MAN HEALTHY, WEALTHY, AND WISE
Arising punctually leads to riches, well being and learning.

EARLY SPRING LEPROSY
A facetious illness preceding the arrival of warm weather.
Spring fever.
[Author's note: crude humor at its worst.]

EARNING YOUR KEEP
A tough job being done well.
As in the case of hens laying eggs at a 90% rate.

EARS LOWERED
Close haircut.

EASY DOES IT
Go slow with this project.

EASY PICKINS
Energy expended in performing a task minor as compared to the rewards.
Smooth sailing.

EATING ME ALIVE
A swarm of dining mosquitoes elicits this remark from the one being dined upon.

EATING MY LUNCH
Refers to someone who continually blocks one's well intended efforts.
As in the case of a competitor who takes customers away from you by unethical means.
"Every time I turn around they start ...."

EATING US OUT OF HOUSE AND HOME

Voracious dependents.
Unwanted boarder.

EAT PEAS WITH A KNIFE

Those who participate in this endeavor consider it a test of skill. Others consider it a breach of etiquette.

E FOR EFFORT

An attempt was made but the results were negative. "All I can do is give you an ...."

EGG ON MY FACE

Embarrassing mistake.

EL ROPE-O

Cheap cigar with an aroma resembling that of a burning rope.

EMPTY SADDLES IN THE OLD CORRAL

Someone is missing.

ENDED UP ON THE CUTTING ROOM FLOOR

Good effort to no avail.

ENGAGE BRAIN BEFORE PUTTING MOUTH IN MOTION

Think before talking.
Advice to one who frequently puts one's foot in one's mouth.

ENOUGH TO THROW TO THE BIRDS

Over production to the point of not being able to get it all harvested. As in the case of a perishable crop of vegetables.

EVEN IF I DO SAY SO MYSELF

Bragging on one's own handiwork.

EVEN STEVEN

Equal amount, share or portion

You go out of the world with the same as when you came in.
"The debt is paid in full and we are now ...."

EVER SO SLOWLY
Pouring molasses in January.
Approaching rain clouds in July.

EVERY DOLLAR A MAN DIES IN DEBT HE'S JUST THAT MUCH AHEAD
Don't fret over borrowed money.

EVERYONE'S OUT OF STEP BUT JOHNNY
Mothers can sometimes see no wrong in their sons.

EVERYTHING BUT THE KITCHEN SINK
As in battle and all weapons firing at will.
"We threw ... at them."

EVERY TIME I TURN AROUND
Seemingly continuous event.
"... there's another bill staring me in the face."

EVERY TIME YOU OPEN YOUR MOUTH YOU STICK YOUR FOOT IN IT
Prone to make verbal mistakes that indicate a lack of intelligence, education or breeding.

EXERCISE IN FUTILITY
Activity for naught. Wasted effort.

EYES ARE PLAYING TRICKS ON ME
Can't believe what I see.

EYES GET BIGGER AND YOUR HEAD GETS LITTLER
Result of watching too much television.

EYES THAT ARE BIGGER THAN HIS STOMACH
Taking more food on the plate than one can consume.
Evident when eating at a cafeteria.
One who leaves a restaurant with left-over food has ....

EXCUSE MY FRENCH

Said before or after a profane expletive.

F

FACT OF THE MATTER IS

My information is more correct than yours.

FAINT DEAD AWAY

Extreme embarrassment as a result of the actions of a close friend or relative.
"If he shows up with that girl I'll just ...."

FAIR UP

A desire for clear skies.
"Wish it would ... a mite so we could go fishing."

FALL APART AT THE SEAMS

Upset, nervous, becoming unglued as a result of pressure, stress, overwork, calamity or havoc.

FALLING-DOWN DRUNK

Very inebriated.

FALLING DOWN ON THE JOB

Poor performance at the work place.

FALLS ON DEAF EARS

One who will not listen to reason. Refuses to accept the truth. "I explain to him the futility of his actions but the effort ...."

FALSE COURAGE

A bottle of alcohol.

FAMOUS LAST WORDS

A statement uttered and then regretted.
A statement one is later sorry for. An inaccurate statement.

His ... were: "It isn't going to get that cold tonight." So we left the plants outside and they all froze.

FAST AND FURIOUS

Attacking a project with extreme enthusiasm. Intense activity directed at a goal.

FAT AND SASSY

Well fixed to the point of being obnoxious. A state of well being.

FAT AS A HOG

Obesity to the extreme.

FAT, DUMB, AND HAPPY

Blissful tranquility as a result of not having enough sense to understand the great problems of the day.

FEELING POORLY

Ill.

FEELS ME GOOD

A close fitting, warm, comfortable garment. "This old sweater may look like heck but it ...."

FEET, DO YOUR STUFF

Running in fright of bodily harm.

FELL OFF

Lost weight; anything that became less productive.

FENCEROW TO FENCEROW

An entire field or farm under cultivation.

FIFTY TWO PICKUP

A game of cards whereby the dealer says, "Have you ever played fifty two pickup?" If the answer is "No," the dealer then throws the whole deck of cards into the air and says, "Pickemup." Usually a short game played only once at the end of a regular card game.

FIFTY TWO TWENTY CLUB

Veterans of World War II and the Korean War were eligible to receive unemployment benefits of twenty dollars per week for one year after discharge.

FIGHT A CIRCLE SAW

Don't take nothin' from nobody. Pugnacious.
"He would ... to get back to her."

FIGHT FIRE WITH FIRE

Eye for an eye, tooth for a tooth. Use same methods as adversary.

FIGHTING A LOSING BATTLE

Struggle against great odds. Trying to get teenagers to identify themselves when they call on the phone. Dealing with a banker who will loan you money if you can prove you don't need it.

FIGHTING MAD

Pushed past the point of sensibility and ready to engage in physical combat in order to uphold one's convictions.

FIGHT NICE

Admonition to children who are squabbling.

FILTHY AS ROT

In need of a bath. As in the case of a child who has been making mud pies.
"Come in here and take a bath, you are as ...."

FINALLY STEPPED IN

Late intervention in a dispute in order to stop a confrontation.

FINANCIALLY EMBARRASSED

Short of funds. Strapped. Monetary resources limited.

FINDERS KEEPERS, LOSERS WEEPERS

The unwritten law about gear left adrift. If you lose it you no longer own it.

FINE FEATHERED FRIENDS

Birds.

"The cat just ate one of my ...."

FINISHING TOUCH

Added refinements to an already fine piece of work.

FIRE IN HER EYES

A woman either angry or passionate.

FIRE IN THE HOLE

Precautionary statement. Preparatory to setting off an explosive.

FIRST COME FIRST SERVED

No reservations. Goods or services supplied in order of appearance of the customer.

FIRST THINGS FIRST

Don't get the cart before the horse. You've got to crawl before you can walk.

FIRST TIME FOR EVERYTHING

Encouraging one to enter a new venture or experience. "But I have never flown before." "There's a ...."

FIRST WHACK AT IT

Head start on the competition.

FIT AS A FIDDLE

Feeling good. Good physical and mental condition. Opposite of "feeling poorly".

FIT FOR A KING

A splendid meal.

FIVE HUNDRED DOLLAR MILLIONAIRE

One who dresses and acts like he has money, but in reality has little.

FIXED UP
Date arranged by a friend.

FLAKE OF HAY
One section or fold from a bale of dried animal forage.

FLASH OF REVELATION
Quickly inspired. Inspiration. Eureka!
"With a ... he wrote the words to the speech without stopping."

FLAT AS A FRITTER
Mashed, rolled out.
As in the case of deflated automobile tire, or a woman devoid of a voluptuous chest, or a possum run over by a truck.

FLYING LOW
High speed land travel.
"He came down the hill in his new car really ...."

FOG SO THICK YOU COULD CUT IT WITH A KNIFE
An exaggeration of a weather condition sometimes called pea soup.

FOO FOO
Fragrances applied to the body such as perfume, after shave lotion or cologne.

FOOT TUB
A low-sided water pail with a capacity of about four gallons. Sometimes used as a hen watering device.

FOR A LITTLE OF NOTHING
Buy cheap.

FOR ALL I KNOW
Accurate information lacking, but implies a ring of truth.
"... she could be sleeping with every man in town."

FOR CRYIN' OUT LOUD
For what reason would you do that.

FOR DAYS ON END
Incessant repetition.
"... we crossed the Pacific traveling by ship."

FOR-E-VER MORE
I am totally amazed. Sometimes preceded by "well."

FORGET MY HEAD IF IT WASN'T GLUED ON
Absentminded self appraiser.

FOR GOOD MEASURE
Additional effort. Adding a little extra to a customer's order after it has been paid for.

FOR NO MORE THAN THEY WAS OF THEM THEY SHORE PUT UP ONE HECK OF A FIGHT
Accolade to an outnumbered enemy.

FOR OLD TIME'S SAKE
To enter into reminiscent activity.
"We took a turn down lovers lane just ...."

FOR SURE FOR SURE
Sincerely true.

FOR THE LIFE OF ME
Trying to remember someone's name or where something needed was stored.
"I can't ... remember his name."

FOUR BUCKLES
Galoshes with quadruple metal fasteners.

FRAIDY HOLE
Storm cellar.

FREE AS A BIRD
Shedding the major encumbrances restricting activity and proceeding with abandon.

FREEZE YOUR TATER OFF
Consequence if one goes out in cold weather without proper clothing.

FRESH AS A DAISY
Pretty, clean, and well groomed.

FRESH BREATH OF SPRING
Beautiful girl enters a room full of men and evokes this remark from an admirer: "Just like a ...."

FRESH OFF THE VINE
Generally used to indicate freshly picked produce. Facetiously used to indicate frequently gathered eggs.

FRIED OUT
Automobile engine inoperative with serious damage.

FRIEND IS VISITING
Flow part of the female menstrual period.

FRIES UP TO NOTHIN'
Store bought bacon that loses much of its mass during the cooking process.

FRITTLE FRATTLE
Nonsense. Usually preceded by "Oh, ..." Variation of "Fiddle-Faddle."

FROGGIE IN THE MEADOW
Cavorting naked child emerging from a bath.

FROM CAN SEE TO CAN'T SEE
Long days in the field from daylight to dark.

[THE] FROST IS ON THE PUMPKIN
Fall cold snap indicating winter is on the way.

FRY ENOUGH UP
Prepare ample supply of food for the occasion.

FULL AS A TICK
Distension of stomach after a big meal.

FULL BOAT
Another term for a full house in a game of poker.
Three of one kind and a pair of another.

FULL BORE
Maximum output
As in the case of an engine operating at full speed.

FULL HAND
Same as hands full.
A lady customer looked at our vegetable truck garden (18 acres) and said: "You surely do have a ...."

FULL OF BEANS
To indicate one who has spoken a falsehood.
"The weatherman called for snow and there's not a flake in sight. He is ...."

FULL SWING
At the peak of activity. "The harvest is in ...."

FUMBLE BUTT
Uncoordinated person.

FUR-LINED JOCK STRAP
This phrase is facetiously used when cold weather arrives.
"It's going to get cold tonight. Got your ... on?"

G

GAG A MAGGOT
Putrid, repulsive, revolting scene.

GAINING ON ME
Work to be done increasing at a rate faster than work accomplished.

GAS GUZZLER
Large automobile with lots of horsepower under the hood.

GEAR HEAD
An unintelligent person with a one track mind. Generally used in reference to a sibling who has just made a monumental blunder.

GENUINE ARTICLE
A truthful sincere person. The "Real McCoy."

GEORGIA ICE CREAM
Missourians' name for grits.
Grits—short for hominy grits. Made from corn. Frequently served with breakfast in southern U.S.A.

GERMAN WORKING STREAK
People of German descent are known for their capacity and inclination for hard work and this is one description.

GET A MOVE ON
Make tracks. Start the project immediately.

GET BACK TO MY RAT KILLING
To go back to work.

GET IN GOOD WITH
To be nice to someone for personal benefit.

GET IN OR GET OUT
Make your bet now. Get off the fence.
As some say: "If you are not a part of the solution, you are a part of the problem."

GET IT OFF YOUR CHEST
Unloading mental burden verbally.

GET IT ON
A way of saying, "get started."

GET IT WHILE IT'S HOT
Time to eat.

GET OFF MY CASE
Quit bothering me with criticism. Leave me alone.

GET ON ABOUT YOUR BUSINESS
Proceed with your own interests and leave me alone.

GET ON MY PONY AND RIDE
I must go.

GET ON THE STICK
Increase productivity. Involve oneself with activities of merit immediately.

GET ON WITH THE BUSINESS AT HAND
The impasse has been going on long enough.
Straying from the course has to come to a stop.

GET ON YOUR PONY AND RIDE
Get out of here and leave me alone.

GET OUT
A mixture of surprise and disbelief and used as a response in conversation. I do not believe you.

GET OUT OF HERE
I don't agree with your idea. You're all wet.

GET OUT OF THIS FIRE TRAP

Has nothing to do with the incendiary nature of a building.
Merely means: Shall we move on to the next place.
Frequently used when bar hopping.
"We've done all the damage we can do here, so let's...."

GET RIGHT DOWN AMONGST THEM

Engage in activity at close range. Grass roots association.
While picking green beans you must ....
In farming you frequently must work at close quarters with plants and animals.

GET SHUT OF

To rid oneself of something not wanted.
A change of ownership to the betterment of the first owner.
This usually refers to a motor vehicle.
"If I had a car that gave me that much trouble I would ... it."
[Note: Some pronounce "shut" as "shud" or "shot."]

GETS IN THERE AND DIGS

A fast accelerating horse such as a well bred quarter horse.
Refers to the action of the hoofs of a horse as they contact the ground during rapid acceleration.

GET THE BIT IN YOUR TEETH

Refers to a horse clamping down on the bridle bit making control difficult and making it easy for the horse to run away with its rider.
Used as an encouragement to charge on with your plans.

GET THE HOTEL BILL OUT OF HERE

Go away and leave me alone.
Also can be used as a statement of intent to leave premises.
"Hotel bill" is a euphemism for hell, like "darn" for damn.
"Let's ...!"

GET THIS

You will not believe this story but it is true. Incredulous.
"Now ..., she told me a tale as to her whereabouts until 3 a.m. that only a moron would believe."

GETTING DOWN TO THE SHORT ROWS
Used when any job nears completion. Winding up, about done. As in the cultivation of a field of irregular shape and one does the point rows last.

GETTING THAT CLOSED IN FEELING
Too long indoors in one place. Cabin fever.

GETTING TO WHERE YOUR PAYCHECK CAN'T SURVIVE THE TRIP HOME
Effects of inflation.

GETTING UP (ALONG) IN YEARS
Elderly.

GETTING UP ON THE WRONG SIDE OF THE BED
Arising in an agitated, angry state of mind.

GETTING WELL IN A HURRY
Making good profit after a period of losses.

GET UP AND FALL DOWN IN MY TRACKS
Overworked.

GET WITH IT
Increase productivity. You are out of step with the times. Put your act together.

GET YOUR HEAD ON THE OTHER END
Said while trying to drive an animal and it stands and faces you.

GIGGLE SILLY
Laughing at the least provocation.
Usually used with reference to a group of young girls.

GIG IT!
An order to rapidly accelerate an automobile.

GIMME FIVE

Greeting to a friend you haven't seen in a long time, which means: Shake hands, pardner.

GINGER PEACHIE

Rosy outlook. Things going well. Just fine.

GIVE A CALF ENOUGH ROPE AND IT WILL HANG ITSELF

Unsupervised activity of youngsters may lead to trouble.

GIVE A LAZY MAN A JOB AND HE'LL FIGURE AN EASIER WAY TO DO IT

Jokingly said to an associate who comes up with a new and better way to accomplish a task.

GIVE CREDIT WHERE CREDIT IS DUE

A compliment sincerely given but sometimes reluctantly.

GIVE HER HECK

A request to accelerate an automobile rapidly.

GIVE HIM AN INCH AND HE WILL TAKE A MILE

Relax rules or controls a little and he'll break them all. Aid to some invites further attachment to some of your assets.

GIVE HIM SOME BREATHING ROOM

Quit pushing or expecting too much.

GIVE IT A WHIRL

Try something new.

GIVES ME A PAIN I CAN'T LOCATE

Irritation at the actions of another.

GIVES ME THE COLD SHIVERS

Prospects of dire circumstances creates this unpleasant sensation of fright.

GIVE THEM HALF A CHANCE

Watch closely or they will give your trouble. "... and they will engage in mischief."

GIVE YOU A RUN FOR YOUR MONEY

Stiff competition.

[THE] GLOVES ARE OFF

Getting down to serious fighting. The situation is getting serious and dire recompense is necessary.

GNAT'S EYEBROW

Exaggerated measure of a minute distance. I came within a ... of making the sale.

GOBS A-PLENTY

Lots of it.

GO BY THE BOOK

Meticulous in the following of commands or regulations.

GO BY THE CODE

Extreme allegiance to one set of values.

GO, CAT, GO

Encouragement to dancers.

GOD'S GIFT TO WOMEN

Egotistical male.

GOES LIKE A HOUSE AFIRE

Fast movement in performance of a task. Speed to the point of a loss in the quality of workmanship.

GOES RIGHT THROUGH YOU

Sharp, bitter cold winter wind. Severe winter wind chill. Nothing between us and the north pole but a barbed wire fence and we're on the wrong side.

GOING FROM BAD TO WORSE

Rapidly deteriorating situation.

GOING JESSE

Female who exhibits uninhibited behavior. "She will do anything, she's a ...."
Sometimes refers to a fast car or a smooth operating piece of machinery like a tractor or a combine.

GOING ROUND AND ROUND

An argument that goes on and on with no change.

GOING TO GIVE HER A LITTLE

Preparing to accelerate as in tightening up a chain when towing another vehicle.

GOING TO HAVE TO PAY GOLD DOLLARS

Price of something in great demand and short supply.

GOING TO HAVE TO SHED

As the day progresses and the activity and temperatures increase, the removal of outer garments is in order. Generally used in spring and fall.

GOING TO HELL IF I DON'T CHANGE MY WAYS

A change from debauchery to the following of the straight and narrow is in order. Is used as a facetious answer to the question: "Where are you going?" "...."

GONE BANANAS

Actions by one who is not using good judgment.

GONE BUT NOT FORGOTTEN

Epitaph. The memory of a departed loved one will live forever.

GONE GOSLIN'

Deceased, dead, missing, disappeared. Also used in anticipation of any failure.

GONE TO STAVES

Bad shape. Can refer to a person in ill health or a machine in bad need of repair.

Basically refers to a wooden barrel that has collapsed due to neglect leaving only a pile of staves from which it was made.

GONNA BE A CHANGE IN THE WEATHER—HOGS IS A CARRYIN' STICKS

Said to a man with a pipe in his mouth.

GONNA BE A CLEAR DAY TOMORROW

All dishes, platters, pots and pans empty at the end of the evening meal.

GONNA BUILD A NEW TOWN—YEA
ONLY ONE BAR—BOO
BE A MILE LONG—YEA
NO BARTENDERS—BOO
ALL BARMAIDS—YEA
BE NO DANCIN' ON THE SMOOCH FLOOR—BOO
BE SMOOCHIN' ON THE DANCE FLOOR—YEA
SELL NO BEER ON SUNDAY—BOO
GIVE IT AWAY—YEA

Young males barroom chant in the 1940s.

GOODBYE CRUEL WORLD

Facetiously suicidal. Joking parting statement when leaving on a mission where there is a certain amount of danger involved.

GOOD CHICKS IN GOOD HANDS

A chicken hatchery man's answer to a customer who comments about how good his baby chicks are doing.

GOOD FOR WHAT AILS YOU

Take your medicine.

GOOD GOLLY MOSES

Expression of amazement at the actions of others.
Can you imagine that?

GOOD GRIEF

Look at that. Now what? What will happen next? Amazing.

[THE] GOOD LORD DOES NOT DEDUCT FROM YOUR ALLOTTED TIME ON EARTH THOSE DAYS SPENT FISHING

Another excuse to go fishing.
The basic meaning of this is that the therapeutic effect of the pursuit of fish will prolong the life of the pursuer.

[THE] GOOD LORD GIVETH AND UNCLE SAM TAKETH AWAY

A slap at the tax collector.
Tax collectors steal from the poor and give to the rich.

[THE] GOOD LORD'S JUST TOUGHENING US UP FOR THE HARD TIMES AHEAD

Used to explain extreme weather such as severe winter blizzard or summer heat wave.

[THE] GOOD LORD WILLING AND THE CREEKS DON'T RISE

I'll be there if I possibly can.

GOOD NIGHT, SLEEP TIGHT AND DON'T LET THE BEDBUGS BITE

Bedtime saying to children.

GOOD RIDDANCE OF (FOR) BAD RUBBISH

Scoundrel leaves town.

GOOD SCOUT

A trusted friend and companion.

GOODY GOODY GUMDROP

Fake praise.

GOODY TWO SHOES

A prissy or overly righteous person.

GOO-GOO BUTTER

Peanut butter.

GO ON ABOUT YOUR BUSINESS
Leave me alone.

GOOSE IT UP
Make it go faster, quickly.

GO PEDDLE YOUR PAPERS
Mind your own business and stay out of mine.

GOT A CATCH IN MY GETALONG
Pain in the lower back restricting activity.
Kink in the back.

GOT A FACE THAT WOULD STOP A CLOCK
Ugly. Unattractive facial features.

GOT A FULL HEAD OF STEAM
Going full blast. We're percolating now.

GOT A LIGHT OUT UPSTAIRS
Mentally unbalanced.

GOT ALL BASES COVERED
Situation well in hand.

GOT A MATCH? (first person)
MY FEET AND (TO) YOUR BREATH (second Person)
Used when someone asks for a light and you feel smart-alecky.

GOT A MEAN STREAK A YARD WIDE
Just plain ornery.

GOT A WAYS TO GO YET
Job far from over.

GOT A WRENCH IN YOUR SOCK?
Asked of a person who is limping.

GOT DANDRUFF, SOME OF IT ITCHES
Mock profanity.

GOT ENOUGH ON HIM TO FILL A BOOK

To know someone well. To know things about another's past that if divulged would be embarrassing.

GOT HIS WIRES CROSSED

Confused, mixed up, crazy.
Someone not following proper procedures.

GO, TIGER

Pursue your dreams with enthusiasm. The girls are out there, make your move.

GOT IN ON THE TAIL END OF IT

Late arrival at a function.

GOT IT MADE IN THE SHADE

Very comfortable. Work done and resting easy. Sitting pretty.

GOT IT WIRED

Dead cinch. Sure thing. Having made extensive preparation, outcome is certain.

GOT MY HEART SET ON IT

Unfulfilled intense desire.

GO TO ROOST WITH THE CHICKENS

Retiring to the bedroom early.
"In boot camp you will ... and arise with the sun."

GOT OTHER FISH TO FRY

Urgent business at another location. Can't be bothered with. Have more important business elsewhere.

GOT SOME BAD ICE LAST NIGHT

Blame for a hangover.

GOT SO SICK WAS AFRAID I WAS GONNA DIE; THEN GOT WORSE SO'S I WAS AFRAID I WASN'T

Very ill indeed.

GOTTA GIT

Goodbye, see you later.
Must get going—am in a hurry.

GOT THE BIG EYE

Eyes bigger than stomach. A person of little means with grandiose ideas. Biting off more than one can chew. Living beyond one's means. A poor person buying a new Cadillac on the installment plan.

GOT THE BLIND STAGGERS

Wandering about without direction or purpose. Frequently used with reference to a person who is intoxicated.

GOT THE CLAMMIES

Cold sweat.

GOT THE HOTS

Female sexually attracted to a male or vice versa.

GOT THEM EATING OUT OF MY HAND

A loyal audience. Unerring followers.

GOT TO HAND IT TO YOU

Compliment for a job well done.

GOT WIND OF IT

Learned information that was to be kept secret.

GOUGE EYE

A very rough place such as a bar in a tough part of town where it is likely a fight might erupt at any time. Sometimes preceded by: "Ol' ...."

GOURD HEAD

Mental capability limited. Often used to describe a younger sibling.

GRAB A ROOT AND GROWL
Take charge of the situation. Jump in with both feet. "Let's go to work! ...."

GRANNY LOW
A truck with transmission in low gear and two speed axle in low range.

GREAT DAY IN THE MORNING
Amazement. So what?
Mother: "Jean, eat your egg."
Jean: "I had a piece of toast."
Mother: "Well ...! Eat your egg anyway."

GREAT WHITE HUNTER
Someone returning from a game procurement mission empty handed.

GREEK GODDESS
A good looking woman. Sometimes used derogatorily about a woman who thinks she is hot stuff.

GREEN AROUND THE GILLS
Sickly appearance.
"You look a little ... this morning."

GREEN AS A GOURD
Absence of ripeness as in produce such as tomatoes, watermelon and pumpkin.
Sometimes used to describe a person who is unenlightened.

[THE] GREEN LIGHT
Permission to proceed.

GRIN AND BEAR IT
Conquering adversity with a smile.

GRIND ME A POUND
Said when someone misses a gear while shifting a motor vehicle transmission resulting in a grating sound.

GRINNING LIKE A POSSUM EATING PERSIMMONS
Guilty smile.

GROWING FOR ALL THEIR WORTH
Rapid growth of a crop or an animal.

GROWING LIKE A WEED
Usually refers to the rapid growth of a child.

GROWS ON YOU
Any person or thing that improves with experience.
Eating something you don't like long enough that you start to like it.

GRUNT AND GROANERS
Professional wrestlers.

GUESS I'LL HAVE TO KNOCK SOME SENSE INTO HIM
A statement made implying physical contact with someone to communicate a message.

GUMMED UP THE WORKS
Fly in the ointment. Impeding progress. Cessation of activity due to external forces.
"We had everything running smoothly and he came along and ...."

GUTLESS WONDER
Lacking courage. Usually a junior military officer lacking intestinal fortitude.

GUT WAGON
Manure spreader.

H

HAIR BENDER
Beauty operator.

HALF-A-NOTION
About ready to act.
"I've got ... to go plant corn if the weather would just cooperate."

HALF PLOWED
Drunk, intoxicated.

HALF-WAY PRESENTABLE
Fairly good appearance. Sometimes used facetiously with reference to a very immaculately groomed and dressed person.

HAND AND MOUTH DISEASE
The affliction of the overweight person.

HANDY AS A POCKET IN A SHIRT
Something very useful.

HANGING OUT
Not doing much. In idle pursuit. To hang around.

HANGING OUT OF THE NEST
Mature offspring still living in parents' home.

HANG IN THERE
Stay with it even though the going may be rough.
A friend calls to console you at your time of loss and his parting statement is "...."

HANG IT ON A NAIL
Due to a condition of hyperopia a person's arms are not long enough to hold a piece of reading material far enough away

for readability. "If I don't have my glasses on I have to ... and back up in order to read the fine print."

HANG IT UP
Quit work for the day.

HANG LOOSE
Keep your cool. Relax but be ready.

HANG ON TO YOUR HAT
Rough road ahead. Aircraft traveling through turbulent air and pilot relays the message "...."

HANG TIGHT
Tenacious. Stay with it, don't give up.

HANKERING AND A-HONING
To yearn for.
"He's just ... for that new car."

HAPPENED TO BE IN THE RIGHT PLACE AT THE RIGHT TIME
By chance one is geographically situated so as to take advantage of a fortunate situation.

HAPPY AS A DEAD PIG IN THE SUNSHINE
Serenity. Blissfully unaware of surrounding influences. Obliviously going one's merry way.

HAPPY AS A LARK
Contented, having a good time.

HAPPY BOTTOM
Nickname for a lady named Gladys.

HARDEE HAR HAR
Fake happiness after a joke has been successfully pulled on you. "... I do not think it is so funny."

HARD PRESSED
Finishing a project under duress. Hard put.

HARD TO COME BY
Difficult to obtain.
"Money is sometimes ...."

HARD WORKING PIECE OF MACHINERY
A man ready, willing and able to perform difficult manual labor.

HASTEN, JASON, BRING THE BASIN—URP, SLOP, BRING THE MOP
Too late to catch the vomit.

HAS THE WORLD BY THE TAIL
Very successful.

HAS TO GO TO THE DEVIL SEVEN TIMES BEFORE IT WILL COME UP
Slow sprouting seeds such as parsley.

HATCHING JACKET
Maternity clothing.

HATED EVERY MINUTE OF IT
Bad experience.
"The movie was so bad I ...."

HAVEN'T GOT THE HANG OF IT YET
Task yet unmastered.

HAVE YOU GOT THAT DOWN?
Verification that one understands your point.

HAVING YOUR NOSE RUBBED IN IT
Being confronted with past mistakes may prevent a reoccurrence in the future.

HAY BELLY
Horse with a distended paunch due to a diet with a grain/ hay imbalance. Too much hay and not enough grain.

HAY FOOT, STRAW FOOT
Military jargon for right and left walking members.

HEADACHE RACK
A protruding extension of a truck bed over the cab designed to increase the capacity for hauling hay. It is in such a position that when inspecting the engine of the truck one's head may come in contact with the extension.

HEAD FOR THE HILLS
Storm's a-brewin'. A disturbance or disaster is imminent.

HEADING OUT
Leaving on a trip.

HEAD ON STRAIGHT
Logical thinker.

HE ALMOST MAKES ME SICK
Can't stand the sight of him.
Person with unlikable ways, personality or actions.

HEART'S IN THE RIGHT PLACE
Benevolent.

HEAVEN FORBID
A way of negating an undesirable behavioral trait.
"... I should never gossip."

HEAVEN'S FULL OF GOOD HOUSEKEEPERS
Let household cleaning tasks go until a later day.
Take a rest from housecleaning chores.
By being too meticulous with the cleanliness of your house, you may be hastening your trip to the grave.
When one says, "Cleanliness is next to Godliness."
Your answer is "...."

HEAVENS TO BETSY
Amazement.

HEAVY WITH CHILD
Pregnant woman in the last trimester.

HEAVY YET
Soil too wet to work.
"You gonna plow today?" "No, the ground's a little ...."

HE CAN DISH IT OUT BUT HE CAN'T TAKE IT
Incapable of bearing the brunt of a joke with grace.
Most practical jokers fit this remark.

HE COULDN'T PUNCH HIS WAY OUT OF A WET PAPER BAG
A discussion of one's pugilistic abilities leads to the conclusion that an adversary is not feared if a fight erupts.

HE DON'T HAVE NO TRUCK WITH US ANYMORE
Someone gone uppity and no longer associates with former friends.

HE DON'T SCARE ME NONE
Appraisal of adversary's abilities.

HEED THE CALL OF NATURE
Defecate or urinate.

HE GETS AROUND
Man about town, with many girl friends; also anyone with lots of contacts.

HE'S GOT A HEAD ON HIM LIKE A CUTWORM
Crafty, intelligent, shrewd.

HE GOT MORE THAN HE BARGAINED FOR
Picking a fight with a superior opponent.

HE GOT RELIGION
After a period of debauchery one sees the light.

HEIGHT OF GLORY
At the peak of success and fame.

HE KNOWS A GOOD THING WHEN HE SEES IT
Astute investor.

HE LEFT HIS CALLING CARD
Territorial animals mark their boundaries with odor—urine often. A visiting animal leaves a similar sign he has been there.
Lingering reminder of one's presence.
Example: Shooting a skunk in the chicken house and the odor lingers for days.

HE LEFT QUITE A MARK ON THIS COUNTRY
Person of great stature who has since passed on.

HE LIES
When false gossip about you reaches your ears, this is the answer.

HE LIES LIKE A RUG
Description of a prevaricator.

HE'LL DO ANYTHING FOR A BUCK
Unprincipled with relation to the acquisition of money.

HELL FOR STOUT
A well built building designed to withstand the worst of conditions. Well braced fence support.

HELLS KA TOOT
Exasperation, anger, frustration. What in tarnation.
"Well ..., what now?"

HELPLESS AS A KITTEN
Pitifully inept.

HELPLESS HANNAH
Inept female.

HELP YOURSELF BY ALL MEANS, YOU KNOW WHERE IT IS

Less than enthusiastic affirmative answer to a request for something such as a drink of water, bottle of pop or beer. The recipient has made this request many times before.

HE PUTS THE "UGH" IN UGLY

Not exactly handsome.

HE QUALIFIES

A good scout. Someone you would ride the trail with. A trusted friend.

HERE GOES NOTHING

Departing on a doubtful mission.

HERE'S LOOKING AT YOU

A toast.

HERE'S YOUR CHARIOT

Assigning drivers to vehicles.

HERE TODAY AND GONE TOMORROW

Unreliable.

HERE WE GO AGAIN

A repeat of some stressful event is in the offing.
[In the spring of 1983, a killer tornado struck the city of Springfield, Mo. Twenty four hours later the tornado alert system sounded again as weary crews were still cleaning up after the first twister. ....]

HE'S A GOOD KID, BUT WHO LIKES KIDS

Even when they're good, they are bad. Sardonic negative appraisal of a person who is not necessarily a child.

HE'S A GOOD'UN

Trusted friend and all round good fellow.

HE SAID SHUT UP AND I THOUGHT HE SAID STAND UP

A bruised friend gives this facetious reply when asked what happened.

HE'S AN ALL RIGHT GUY

Good friend.

HE'S AS SORRY AS THEY COME

A person of little ambition or accomplishment resulting in his being held in low esteem by his peers.

Worthless individual in the eyes of the person making the statement.

HE'S BEEN LIKE A FATHER TO ME

Helpful older male. A sincere compliment about a male person of no blood relation who, through compassion and helpfulness, becomes a parent figure.

HE'S GOING AT IT LIKE HE'S KILLING SNAKES

Attacking a job with excessive fervor. Excited approach to an activity. Wildly entering into feverish activity with little result.

HE'S GOT A LOT OF STUFF AROUND HIM

A person with great wealth and much property.

HE'S GOT A LOT TO LEARN

Someone who behaves confidently when caution is needed.

HE'S GOT AN HONEST EYE

Looks like a fair dealer to me.

HE'S GOT A SHORT FUSE

Bad temper. Easily provoked into a fight.

HE'S GOT MORE MONEY THAN CARTER'S GOT PILLS

Wealthy.

Refers to Carter's Little Liver Pills that were produced in great quantities.

HE'S GOT THE COIN
Well off financially. Money available for investment. High ratio of liquid assets.

HE'S RIGHT IN THAT REGARD
Generally wrong, but in this case offers a correct assessment.

HE'S WORSE THAN A SHEEP-KILLING DOG
Bad hombre.

HE WAS SO SCARED HE HEARD THE SOUND OF THE SAME BULLET TWICE, ONCE WHEN IT PASSED HIM AND AGAIN WHEN HE PASSED IT
Jokingly refers to a person who is easily frightened.

HE WHO HESITATES IS LOST
Grasp an opportunity immediately for it may never come your way again.
Good advice in the pursuit of business or love.

HE WHO LAUGHS LAST LAUGHS LONGEST
Critics may not be happy with your success but you will be.
Winning on the last volley.

HE WOULD ARGUE WITH A FENCE POST IF IT WOULD TALK BACK
Always willing to debate an issue.

HE WOULDN'T GIVE ME THE TIME OF DAY
Not exactly sympathetic to your cause.

HE WOULD ROLL OVER IN HIS GRAVE
Shameful activities by relatives or associates after the departure of one's soul from earth.
"If he could see the actions of his widow ...."

HEY, YOUR HORN WORKS—TRY YOUR LIGHTS
Retort to someone honking automobile horn incessantly.

HIDE, HAIR, AND ALL
Cleaned the platter. "Ate the whole thing ...."

HIGH ON THE TOTEM POLE
Person with an elevated position in the hierarchy.

HIS DOBBER IS DOWN
Feeling poorly. Mentally dejected.

HIS FATHER TAUGHT HIM HOW TO SWIM, BUT THE PROBLEM WAS GETTING OUT OF THE SACK WITH THE ROCK IN IT
Said of any person successful in performance.
Refers to the cat population control method of drowning in a sack with a rock in it.

HIS HAND IS NEVER FAR FROM A BOTTLE
One description of an alcoholic.

HIS TIME WAS UP
Death.

HIT A LICK
Good results as in a bumper crop or making a deal involving a nice profit.

HIT ME LIKE A TON OF BRICKS
Unexpected calamity.

HIT THE JUG
Excessive consumption of alcoholic beverages.

HIT THE SILK
Jump out of an aircraft in flight with a parachute.
[While flying over the Gulf of Mexico in a twin engine U.S. Navy SNB Aircraft in 1949, our right engine caught fire. After efforts to extinguish the fire failed the pilot said, "Get ready to ...." We donned parachutes but the fire was put out before we had to jump.]
Some use this phrase in place of, "go to bed."

HIT THEM WHERE IT HURTS
Adversary may be more quickly defeated by finding his Achilles heel.

HOBBY THAT GOT OUT OF HAND
Avocation that grew into a vocation.

HOCK A LUNGER
Expel phlegm.

HOG IT IN
Planting a crop without proper seed bed preparation. Planting seeds in soil with an excess amount of moisture present.

HOLD HER, NEWT, SHE'S A-RARING
Said to one who is embroiled in a violent uncontrolled situation. As in the case of roping a calf and becoming entangled in the rope, and then one is buffeted about.

HOLD STILL
Remain immobile. Said to a horse while trimming hooves. As a young boy squirms under the barber's scissors and comb, his mother says, "...."

HOLD THE PHONE
Stop right where you are until I find out what happened. Cease activities temporarily.

HOLLER AFORE THEY'RE A-HURTING
People with the personality trait of feeling sorry for themselves. They complain about bad things that are not about to happen.

HOLY SAPPHIRE
Amazement.
"... look at that dress she is wearing."

HOME FREE
Difficult task completed without incident. Results could have been disastrous but were not.

HOME IS WHERE THE HEART IS
Families make a home out of a house. Often used on needlepoint projects.

HONEST AS THE DAY IS LONG
Truthful, trustworthy.

HONESTY IS THE ROAD TO STARVATION
Told to me by a cohort in 1965, and at times, it seems true. It's a disillusion comment on the way the world works.

HONEY, DO
Jobs around the house a wife asks the husband to perform.

HONEY GOOSUM
Mixture of bee nectar and butter.

HONOR AMONG THIEVES
Code of ethics of the criminal element.
There is no such thing as a totally honest or totally dishonest person.

HOOK, LINE AND SINKER
Gullible. Believed the whole false story.
"He swallowed the story ...."

HOPE LIGHTNING DON'T STRIKE HERE, IT'LL GET THE WHOLE BUNCH
Said to a group of persons who should be dispersed elsewhere at work.

HOP TO IT
Begin at once.

HORSE BISCUITS
Equine feces.

HORSE CORN
Roasting ears made from field corn as opposed to sweet corn.

HORSE OF A DIFFERENT COLOR
A different situation requiring new tactics.

HOT AND COLD RUNNING BLONDS
Facetious plumbing fixtures in a bachelor's apartment.

HOT AS A PISTOL
Very heated from overexertion in the heat of the day.

HOT DAMN
News of good luck.
"... my horse won going away by three lengths."

HOTTER THAN A FIRECRACKER
A streak of good luck as in gambling.
An actor or musician whose talents and popularity make him in great demand.

HOTTER THAN BLUE BLAZES
Extremely warm humid day.
Suffering from high temperature.

HOT TO GO
Ready to move on with the project. Sometimes used to describe readiness for activity. Occasionally said as individual letters, "Ho-to-go."

HOW ARE YOU FEELING? (first person)
WITH MY FINGERS (second person)
Answer is made by one who had been ill but is feeling better to the point of being clever.

HOW DO YOU LIKE YOUR EGGS? (first person)
OH I LIKE 'EM (second person)
It makes no difference how you cook them, I will eat.

HOW IN THE WORLD ARE YOU?
A sincere inquiry into one's well being. Used when meeting someone after a period of time.
More serious than, "How ya doin'?"

HOW IN THE WORLD
Questioning an act, statement, or accomplishment.
"... will they be able to pay for that new home?"

"... could he have said that about her?"
"... did he get elected to be the mayor?"

HOWLING MAD
Very irritated.

HOW LUCKY CAN YOU GET?
Good fortune befalls one.

HOWLY GROWLIES
Hunger pangs.

HOWLY GROWLING AROUND
Out on the town. Bar hopping.

HOW MUCH MORE CAN WE TAKE?
Despair after a series of calamities.

HOW'S THAT GRAB YOU?
What is your opinion of that proposal?

HOW'S THEM APPLES?
That's my opinion, what do you think of it? These are the facts, like it or not.

HOW'S THE WORLD TREATING YOU? (first person) BETTER THAN I DESERVE, THANK YOU (second person)
The first phrase is used to greet a friend you haven't seen in quite some time. The second person's answer is used if things are going exceptionally well.

HOW SWEET IT IS
Appraisal of the successful outcome of a mission.

HOW'S YOUR PULSE A-BEATIN'?
Inquiring into one's health.

HOW THE OTHER HALF LIVES
A visit to the better part of town lets you see ....

HOW WOULD YOU FEEL ALL SHUT UP?
When a person tells another to "shut up", this is the response: "...."

HOW YOU STACKIN'?
What is your condition?
Are you doing alright?

HUFFING AND A PUFFING
Hurrying. This occurs after a period of running in circles.

HULLY GULLY
Said as an enticement to lady luck just before rolling the dice.
An expression of mild surprise.

HUMAN DYNAMO
Energetic workaholic.

HUNG UP HIS SPURS
Quit the job. Retired.

HURRY BACK
Said very fast, almost as one word, as one leaves your domicile. Please return as soon as you can as I will miss you while you are gone.
Variation: "Take your time going, but ...."

HURRY UP AND WAIT
Standard routine in the military.

HUSH, YOU'LL RAISE THE DEAD
Usually said to children who are making too much noise.

HYPED UP
Overactive, exuberant, excited.

I

I AIN'T AFRAID OF WORK—I CAN LAY DOWN RIGHT BESIDE IT AND GO TO SLEEP

Self appraisal of one's ability to shun duties with a clear conscience.

I CAN DREAM, CAN'T I?

Window shopping with no money in your jeans.

I CAN HOLD MY HEAD UP AGAIN

Cleared of shameful charges.

I CAN MEND ANYTHING BUT A BROKEN HEART

Confident repairman's credo.

I CAN ROW A BOAT—CANOE?

One of those nonsensical statements used by the young of heart as a time filler in a frivolous conversation.
Canoe in this case is a substitute for, "Can you."

I CAN TAKE ANYTHING YOU CAN DISH OUT

Not easily frightened. Confidence built on past experience.

I CAN'T GET OVER THAT

Amazement.

I COULD EAT A BARREL OF IT

Appraisal of a personal gustatory delight.
Exaggerated statement intended to show extreme preference for a food.
"... watermelon, cantaloupe and tomatoes."

I COULD JUST BITE NAILS

Angry to the point of exasperation.

I COULD WRING YOUR NECK

Dissatisfaction with the actions of another to the point of physical retribution, but the act is never carried out.

I DEAL DIRECT

Congregations, presided over by priestly persons, are not necessary to communicate with the Almighty.
Open channel to the front office.
Purchases involving the elimination of the middleman.

I DIDN'T JUST FALL OFF THE TURNIP TRUCK

Not as naive as you think.

I DIDN'T LOSE ANYTHING OVER THERE

Not wishing to make a return visit.

IDIOT STICK

A person with a tendency toward abnormal behavior.

IDIOT STICK TIME—DAYLIGHT SAVINGS TIME GOD'S TIME—STANDARD TIME

One hill farmer's evaluation of the machinations of man with regard to time setting for his convenience. Cows and chickens get up on God's time.

IDLENESS BREEDS CONTEMPT

The working person has little praise for the able bodied lazy.

I DON'T CARE WHAT THEY SAY, THAT'S PRETTY

Beauty is in the eye of the beholder.
This is usually said while observing one's own handiwork.

I DON'T CARE WHAT THEY CALL ME AS LONG AS THEY CALL ME IN TIME FOR SUPPER

Immune to brickbats as long as they don't interfere with the vittles.

I DON'T DEAL IN THAT TRUCK

Said by one who does not deal in shoddy merchandise.

I DON'T GET ULCERS, I HIRE THEM

One method of healthy management.

I DON'T KEEP A BELL ON HIM

Answer when asked the whereabouts of a person you have no control over and could care less.

I DON'T KNOW HIM FROM ADAM

A stranger. A person not seen for a long time and his change in appearance renders him unrecognizable.

I DON'T KNOW VERY MUCH, BUT WHAT I KNOW I KNOW GOOD

One with no vast storehouse of knowledge, but what is lacking in depth is made up for in thoroughness.

I DON'T KNOW WHERE YOU ARE COMING FROM

I do not understand your point of view.
We are not communicating on the same level.

I DON'T MIND TELLING YOU

Strong feelings about a subject and willing to talk about it. Disagreement with the statement or actions of another.

I DON'T WANT TO BE A MILLIONAIRE—I JUST WANT TO LIVE LIKE ONE

Credo of the credit card jet set.

I'D RATHER BE A BIG DUCK IN A LITTLE PUDDLE THAN A LITTLE DUCK IN A BIG PUDDLE

Satisfied with success in a small town.

I'D RATHER BE ON THE OUTSIDE LOOKING IN THAN ON THE INSIDE LOOKING OUT

Confinement is unpopular. A reason for keeping one's nose clean. Refers to incarceration in a jail cell.

I'D RATHER OWE IT TO YOU THAN BEAT YOU OUT OF IT

One answer to a debt collector. I can't pay you now but will as soon as I can.

I DRAWED DOWN ON IT

Getting ready (to act) for action.

Refers to the drawing of bead with a rifle preparatory to firing.

IF A CHICKEN STAYS OUT IN THE RAIN IT MEANS IT'S GOING TO RAIN ALL DAY

A chicken will run to the chicken house at the first drops of a shower. If the rain continues, it will go back out to forage for the rest of the day.

IF A FROG DIDN'T HOP IT WOULDN'T BUMP ITS BOTTOM

To venture forth in uncharted waters sometimes brings encounters with rocky shoals.

IF A FROG HAD WINGS IT WOULDN'T BUMP IT BOTTOM WHEN IT HOPPED

Speculation as to outcome under a set of unrealistic circumstances.

First person: "If I just had a million dollars."

Second person: "...." (Your chances of getting a million dollars is about the same as a frog growing wings.)

IF AT FIRST YOU DON'T SUCCEED, TRY, TRY AGAIN

Persist until success is accomplished.

I FEEL FOR YOU, BUT I CAN'T REACH YOU

Sorry, I will be of no help to you in your predicament.

IF HE HAD A BRAIN, HE WOULD BE DANGEROUS

Derogatory remark about one's lack of common sense.

IF HE'S WORTH HIS SALT

Questioning one's ability to carry his share of the load.

IF I KNEW THEN WHAT I KNOW NOW

Hindsight is almost always 100%.

IF I SNOOZE I LOSE
An opportunity that could be very beneficial may be lost if you are not alert.

IF IT AIN'T ONE DARN THING IT'S ANOTHER
A series of defeats or mishaps brings this statement.

IF IT FEELS GOOD, DO IT
Credo of the uninhibited.

IF IT'S ALL THE SAME TO YOU
Assuming it makes no difference. Asking if it makes a difference. "... I could do without that loud music."

IF IT WAS A SNAKE, IT WOULD BITE YOU
Telling someone who is looking for something that it is right under his nose.

IF I'VE GOT TO CARRY A LANTERN, I'M GOING TO CARRY IT IN THE MORNING
If there is not enough daylight in the day to get the work all done, starting early is the preference of some.

IF I WAS A BETTING MAN
Preface to a statement indicating a sure thing.
"... I'd wager you can't whip me."

IF NOT, WHY NOT?
What is your excuse?

IF PANTS FOR AN ELEPHANT WERE TEN CENTS A PAIR, I COULDN'T BUY TIGHTS FOR A FLEA
Poor financial condition.
"I'm so poor ...."

IF PEOPLE WOULD JUST CLAMP DOWN ON THEIR KIDS
Stating a solution to juvenile misbehavior.

IFS, ANDS OR BUTS

Trying to elicit a decisive answer.
"Don't give me any ..., just a straight answer."

IF SILENCE IS GOLDEN—I'M POVERTY STRICKEN

Self assessment by a talkative person.
Answer when someone says, "Silence is golden".

IF THE SHOE FITS, WEAR IT

Used to express the idea that if a derogatory characterization of you is correct, then accept it.

IF THE SHOE WAS ON THE OTHER FOOT

Figuratively speaking, put yourself in my place.

IF WORSE COMES TO WORST

Action is withheld until the very last minute to allow time for conditions to improve. A course of action is planned in the event conditions do not improve.

IF YOU ALWAYS CUT AWAY FROM YOURSELF, YOU WILL NEVER CUT YOURSELF

Admonition by elders to a youngster learning proper use of a knife.

IF YOU CAN DO, YOU DO
IF YOU CAN'T DO, YOU TEACH

Questioning the ability of educators.

IF YOU CAN SEE ONE AT ALL WHEN THEY COME UP, THEY ARE TOO THICK

Advice as to when to thin the turnip plant population. Turnip seeds and seedlings are so tiny compared to the mature plant, that seemingly excessive thinning is sometimes necessary in order to get good-sized turnips.

IF YOU CAN'T DO THE TIME, DON'T DO THE CRIME

Be prepared to suffer the consequences when you consider breaking the law.

IF YOU CAN'T STAND THE HEAT, DON'T LIGHT THE CANDLE

Similar to Harry S. Truman's saying: "If you can't stand the heat, stay out of the kitchen."

If you become embroiled in a controversy, be prepared to take the consequences. Be prepared to accept criticism graciously for your actions when entering a controversial situation.

IF YOU COULD BUY HIM FOR WHAT HE'S WORTH AND SELL HIM FOR WHAT HE THINKS HE'S WORTH, YOU'D MAKE A MILLION DOLLARS

Derogatory appraisal of an egoist.

IF YOU DON'T LIKE IT, YOU CAN LUMP IT

Your opinion of my action is of no concern to me.

IF YOU DON'T LIKE THE WEATHER HERE IN THE OZARKS, JUST WAIT FIVE MINUTES

Can be used in any area of rapidly changing atmospheric conditions.

IF YOU HAVE TIME TO SPARE, GO BY AIR

Overheard in a fog-shrouded airport waiting room.

Did you ever wonder why airport waiting rooms are so large?

IF YOU HAVE TROUBLE GETTING ALONG WITH YOUR NEIGHBORS AND WANT TO KNOW WHY—GO LOOK IN A MIRROR

Go to great lengths to keep peace with people of close proximity to your residence. You may be the one at fault if you don't get along with them.

IF YOU NEED A HELPING HAND, YOU'LL FIND ONE AT THE END OF YOUR ARM

Someone asks for help who, in the past, has refused to lend a hand. Your answer is: "...."

IF YOU'RE EVER DOWN BY THE RIVER, DROP IN
Sardonic humor. I don't like you.

IF YOU'RE TOO BUSY TO GO FISHING, YOU'RE TOO BUSY
Employment is no excuse for being denied the pursuit of Pisces.

IF YOU'RE WAITING ON ME, YOU'RE KILLING TIME
Ready to go.

IF YOU'VE GOT IT, FLAUNT IT
Don't be shy or reluctant to admit you are outstanding in your appearance or ability.

IF YOU WANT ANYTHING DONE RIGHT, DO IT YOURSELF
Seldom will a person perform a task to another's expectation.

I GIVE YOU FAIR WARNING
Retribution imminent if conditions between us worsen.

I GOT SOME SWEET CORN FROM YOU YESTERDAY, BUT IT DIDN'T KEEP—I ATE IT ALL
Compliment, disguised at first.

I GOT TO WALK OVER THE SAME ROCKS YOU DO
My job is just as rough as yours.

I GUARANGODDAMNTEEYA
I feel quite sure of the outcome.
I can assure you the results will be as I predicted.

I HATE HIM WITH A PASSION
Extreme dislike.

I HAVE NO QUARREL WITH A MAN WHO SELLS FOR LESS, FOR HE OF ALL PEOPLE SHOULD KNOW WHAT HIS PRODUCT IS WORTH

Use quality to compete instead of price.

I HEERED YOU WHEN YOU DRIV' UP

Said to someone when you have heard enough, in place of "shut up!".

I JUST HAVE A SNEAKING FEELING

Can't put my finger on it, but there is reason for suspicion.

I KID YOU NOT

Seriously, I mean what I say.
"...; weather like this causes the use of a lot of wood just to keep warm."

I KNOW HOW TO GET YOUR GOAT (first Person)
HOW? (Second Person)
WATCH WHERE YOU TIE IT (first Person)

"Get your goat," means to perturb.
This is an example of secondary colloquialism.
One must know the meaning of the first saying in order to understand the humor of the second.

I KNOW ON REASON IT'S TRUE

Good reliable source makes this information very likely to be accurate.

I'LL BE A HORN-SWOGGLED TOAD

Acute exasperation.

I'LL BEAT YOU SOMETHIN' UNMERCIFUL

Threat of dire consequences if our relations do not improve.

I'LL CLIMB YOUR FRAME

Retribution with fisticuffs imminent.

I'LL DANCE AT YOUR WEDDING
Mock payment for a favor.
When someone does something for you, instead of an offer of monetary reward, you say: "...."

I'LL EAT YOU ALIVE
Competitive bragging.

I'LL FIX YOUR WAGON
A threat to get even or settle an old score.

I'LL FLY ANYWHERE WITH YOU IF YOU WILL LET ME KEEP ONE FOOT ON THE GROUND
Acrophobia pun.

I'LL GET TO IT DIRECTLY
Procrastination.

I'LL GIVE YOU A HAIR LIP
Warning—I'm gonna swat you.
Variations: knuckle sandwich, fat lip.

I'LL JERK A KNOT IN YOUR TAIL
Warning of dire consequences.
"If you don't quit pestering me, ..."

I'LL SEE TO THAT
Will make sure it is taken care of.

I'LL TELL THE COCKEYED WORLD
Boastful pronouncement.
I will voice my opinion whether you like it or not.
"... if we don't vote in a new president with different policies, this country is going to hell in a handbasket."

I'LL TELL YOU ONE THING
Stern pronouncement coming up.
"..., you are not man enough to take her away from me."

I'LL TRY ANYTHING ONCE
Entering into a new experience where there is a possibility of danger or chance of failure.

I'LL WHIP THE SNOT OUT OF YOU
Be careful or you are going to get it.
"You better quit kicking my dog around or ...."

I LOVE EVERY BONE IN HER BODY
Infatuation.

I'M A LITTLE AFRAID OF THAT
Suspicion.

I'M A LOVER, NOT A FIGHTER
Make love, not war.

I'M AS TIRED AS IF I HAD WORKED ALL DAY
Used in two ways: Jokingly used in the case of really working hard all day. In the second way, one has really done nothing all day and is tired.

I'M A WARM WEATHER DUCK
Dislikes frigid weather.
"How do you like this first cold and snow of the season?" "I don't like it, ..."

I MAY NOT LOOK ANY BETTER, BUT I DO SMELL A LOT BETTER
Coming out of the shower after a long hard day of work.

I'M NOT THAT MUCH OF AN EXPERT, BUT
Someone asks your advice on something of which you know little, but you go ahead and give your opinion anyway.

I'M SO FAR BEHIND I THINK I'M IN FRONT
Considerably off schedule as one proceeds through the day of work. Relates to lapping in racing.

I'M THE WORLD'S WORST

A degrading appraisal of one's own abilities.
"... at remembering names."

I'M WITH YOU

I agree with your position on the subject.
Will accompany you on the trip.

IN A DIFFERENT WORLD

Describing a mild nonconformist.

IN A RUT

Bogged down in the quagmire of repetitive endeavor.

IN A TIGHT

Binding situation. Payment due and funds short.

IN BAD STRAITS

Poor condition. Strapped.

IN CASE

Hay in the field which, due to high moisture content, is too damp to bale. Mold or spontaneous combustion can occur if hay is stored in the barn in this condition.

IN CIRCULATION

Available and looking for a mate.
After going steady for a period of time there is a break in relations and both parties are back ....

INDEPENDENT AS A HOG ON ICE

Refers to a person or animal who is indifferent to the wishes of others. Headstrong. Refers to hogs walking on ice. They sometimes slip and fall down and will just lay there resisting all efforts to help them.

I NEEDED THAT LIKE I NEED A HOLE IN THE HEAD

Misfortune.

I NEVER SHED A TEAR

The expectations are that sadness will result, but the opposite (happiness) prevails.
"With their departure ...." (Unwelcome guests leaving.)

IN HOG HEAVEN

Extremely happy due to a very enjoyable experience.

IN LIKE FLYNN

Got it made.
To score with a female.

IN MY LITTLE PEA BRAIN

Self ridicule of one's own intelligence.
My opinion, no matter how little thought it took to form it.
Low self esteem.

INTEREST GOES ON WHILE YOU'RE SLEEPING

For borrowers and lenders alike.
Ask yourself which position you would rather be in before you borrow money.

IN TOTAL COMMAND OF THE SITUATION

Everything's under control.

INTO THE MOUTH AND AROUND THE GUMS— LOOK OUT, BELLY, HERE SHE COMES

A toast with a drink that is low quality.

INVESTMENT IN A BETTER SON-IN-LAW

Cost of braces on the teeth of a teenage girl.

IRISH AS PATTY'S PIG

The name, Kelly.

IRON LUNGS

Cheerleaders.

I SADLY FEEL SOMETHING IS DREADFULLY WRONG

Someone long overdue. Premonition of disaster.

I SAW A SAW IN ARKANSAS THE BIGGEST SAW I EVER SAW
I NEVER SAW A SAW SAW LIKE THE SAW I SAW SAW IN ARKANSAS
I'D SAW MY WOOD ON ANY SAW I EVER SAW IN ARKANSAS SAW

Homonymous play with words.

I SCREAM
YOU SCREAM
WE ALL SCREAM
FOR ICE CREAM

Hot weather chant.

I SEEM TO RECALL

Bringing up something in one's past that he does not want to hear. Recollection of a bad act or words.
Prelude to collection of a debt. "... that your note is overdue."

I SHOULDN'T HAVE DONE THAT

Mused by man viewing pregnant girlfriend.

I SPECK NOT

Constipated fly statement.
Short for "I expect not."

IT AIN'T ALL THAT BAD

Cheer up, things could be worse.

IT AIN'T ALL THAT MUCH FUN

Disagreeable task that is necessary to perform.
A fair to middlin' bad experience.

IT AIN'T WHAT YOU WANT, IT'S WHAT YOU GET THAT MAKES YOU FAT

Goals are just goals until they are accomplished. Desires and procurement are two different things. Used in a case where a child wants something not possible to obtain.

ITCHEE KITCHEE KOO
Said while giving the baby a chuck under the chin.

IT DID CROSS MY MIND
Fleetingly considering an evil deed. Consideration of a thought, but not seriously.

IT DOESN'T LOOK GOOD
Prognosis bleak, death imminent.

IT FEELS SO GOOD OUT—BELIEVE I'LL LEAVE IT OUT
A stroll on a warm summer evening by a male to answer the call of nature elicits this remark.

IT FELL ON A PAPER
Picking up and eating a piece of food that had fallen to the bare floor and then one says, "...."

IT HAPPENS IN THE BEST OF FAMILIES
Said in a consoling manner to someone who has related a tale of woe.

I THOUGHT YOU LEFT THE COUNTRY
Greeting to a person not seen in a long time.

IT'LL ALL COME OUT IN THE WASH
Controversy settled by arbitration.

I TOLD YOU SO WAS A VERY ODD FELLOW HIS HEAD WAS ROUND AND HIS BELLY WAS MELLOW
I know you told me so—so what!
When someone brings up an embarrassing mistake you have made and says, "I told you so." Your answer is, "...."

I TRUST HIM ABOUT AS FAR AS I CAN SPIT
Integrity in doubt.

IT'S A DEAD CINCH
Got it wired. Locked in. Will happen for sure.

IT'S A GREAT LIFE IF YOU DON'T WEAKEN
Strength to withstand the problems of life will lend a helping hand in the quest for happiness. Trial and tribulation will threaten happiness, but don't give up.

IT'S ALL OVER FOR THEM
No survivors of a plane crash.

IT'S ALL PART OF THE GAME
Routinely bilking someone out of his money. Some businessmen cheating on their income taxes consider that ....

IT'S ALL YOURS
Turning a job over to someone else.

IT'S BEEN A LONG DAY
Making mistakes in the afternoon, one makes the excuse ....

IT'S CLEAN DIRT
Clothing soiled while engaged in labor tilling the soil.

IT'S DONE DONE NOW
Act complete—result irreversible.

IT'S GOT A KICK LIKE A MULE
Highly intoxicating alcoholic beverage.

IT'S HIGH TIME YOU DID
Obligation long overdue.

IT'S HOME TO YOU
Returning to childhood territory.

IT'S JUST WIRED TOGETHER
Disdain for someone's old decrepit automobile. Anything in use but barely usable.

IT'S NOT WHAT YOU KNOW, BUT WHO YOU KNOW
One avenue to success. This is especially true in politics and some corporate environments.

IT'S YOUR BABY

You are now responsible for the project.

IT'S YOUR NICKEL

Expense born by another for an activity you both share in. "You called me long distance. ... talk as long as you like."

IT'S YOUR OWN BREATH BLOWING BACK IN YOUR FACE

Answer when someone says you stink.

IT WAS SO CROWDED YOU COULDN'T CUSS A CAT WITHOUT GETTING HAIR IN YOUR MOUTH

Description of a large gathering of persons in close quarters.

IT WILL FLAT DO IT

A machine capable of good performance.

IT WILL PASS

Hunger pang and not mealtime yet.

IT WON'T BE LONG NOW

Expectation of the result of an operation or set of circumstances.

I'VE GOT AN IN THERE

Privy to inside information.

I'VE HAD IT UP TO HERE

(A hand motion across the throat.)
A belly full of your antics has me in such a state of exasperation that I caution you to desist at once.

I'VE NEVER SEEN THE LIKE

Consternation.

I VIEW THAT WITH MIXED EMOTIONS

Finding that your income has risen to the point that you are in a higher tax bracket.
Frost brings an end to vegetable harvest in the fall, but also ends the income derived therefrom.

I WANTED IT (TO) SO BAD I COULD TASTE IT
Intense desire.

I WAS BORN LAZY
Reaction to a comment about one's ability to shun work.

I WAS FOUGHT EVERY STEP OF THE WAY
A difficult task completed after much interference from adversaries.

I WAS SO SCARED I HID IN MY MOTHER'S APRON POCKET
A way of saying that I was a shy child.

I WOULDN'T GIVE YOU A NICKEL FOR HIM IF YOU GAVE ME FOUR CENTS CHANGE
I think this fellow is a despicable character.

I WOULDN'T GIVE YOU TWO CENTS FOR DINNER
Said as one leaves a cafeteria or restaurant after a very good meal.

I WOULDN'T SWEAR TO IT
Fairly, but not absolutely certain.

I'Z A-FIXIN TO
Will get to it directly. Getting ready to start a task. Procrastination.
"The yard needs mowing and there you sit, drinking beer and watching television." "...."

J

JACK IT UP AND PUT A NEW ONE UNDER IT
Automobile too far gone to rebuild.

JEWISH PENICILLIN
Chicken soup.

JOY JOY
Fake happiness.
Said to oneself at the arrival of a disliked person.
"... look who's here."

JUICING TIME
The time of day when cows are normally milked.

JUMPED ALL OVER HIM
Verbal abuse for an infraction.

JUMPIN' GEE HOSSAFAT
What a surprise. Look at that. Amazement. Bewildered at the actions of another.

JUMPING ON THE BAND WAGON
Attaching oneself to a cause after victory is apparent.

JUST ABOUT BUT NOT QUITE
Ninety-nine percent true. Money can ... buy anything.

JUST A-ITCHIN'
Fit to be tied.
Rarin' to go.

JUST BETWEEN YOU AND ME AND THE GATEPOST
Gossip forthcoming.
I am going to tell you a secret and don't tell a soul.
"... I think he is a pompous, egotistical bigmouth."

JUST EATING IT UP
Accepting praise with abandon.

JUST FOR GREENS
The heck of it. Do it for kicks.
No apparent reason for the act.

JUST GOING TO LEAVE IT AT THAT
Exhaustion or lack of daylight dictates that a job must remain unfinished temporarily.

JUST HAD A FEELING
Knew it was going to happen.

JUST HAVING A PICNIC
Animal or person doing something he should not, but enjoying it very much.
Horses in the cornfield.
Worm eating its way through an ear of sweet corn.

JUST KEEPING THEM HONEST
Locking the door to an automobile or abode.

JUST LIKE A DOSE OF (EPSOM) SALTS
Rapid passage. Job quickly finished. Compares action to catharsis or purgation.

JUST LIKE MONEY IN THE BANK
A sure thing.

JUST LIKE ONE BIG HAPPY FAMILY
A group closely associated in harmony, but not related.
A well run office is ....

JUST LIKE RIDING A BICYCLE—YOU NEVER FORGET HOW
Skills once acquired are not ever totally forgotten.

JUST LIKE SHOOTING DUCKS IN A BARREL
Taking unfair advantage. A sure thing.

JUST LIKE TAKING CANDY FROM A BABY

Easy task. Sometimes used to indicate the act of legally separating people from their money by appealing to their greed.

Example: Unethical investment schemes.

JUST LIKE THE BIG BOYS DO

A low budget operation putting out a high quality product.

JUST LIKE TWO PEAS IN A POD

A pair that look or do exactly alike.

JUST LIKE WATER ROLLING OFF A DUCK'S BACK

Task easily performed.

JUST MY LUCK

Misfortune seems to follow me around.

JUST WHAT THE DOCTOR ORDERED

Solution solves the problem perfectly. Help in the time of need.

"It was a hot July afternoon when the combine broke down in the middle of harvest and wife arrives with a cold beer ...."

JUST WHISTLE

An offer of assistance.

"If I can be of help to you ...."

K

KAMEEN BOX
Closet under a frame-suspended masonry flue.
Chimney closet.

KATY, BAR THE DOOR
Connotation relating to wild behavior.
Someone arriving at a party who has a reputation for raucous behavior gets this greeting.
"..., here comes ________."

KEEP A CIVIL TONGUE IN YOUR MOUTH
Speak to your elders with respect.

KEEPS COMING BACK FOR MORE
Masochistic.

KEEPS YOU HUMPING
Urgent work that keeps you busy.

KEEPS YOU ON YOUR TOES
Making ends meet during trying times.
Seven children to support ....

KEEP THE FAITH, BABY
Don't give up.

KEEP YOUR BELLY FROM GROWLING
Between-the-meals snack.

KEEP YOUR NOSE CLEAN
Admonition to stay out of trouble with the law.

KEEP YOUR SHIRT ON
Admonition to an impatient person.
Be patient, we will proceed as soon as it is feasible.

KICKED A SLAT OUT OF MY CRADLE WHEN I FIRST HEARD THAT ONE

A joke as old as the hills.
Relates to the use of an old cliché or joke.

KICKING THE PAIL AGAIN

Describing a person who repeatedly stirs up a stink about a situation.

KICK OVER THE HAME STRAP

Exuberant.
The hame strap is the part of the harness on a work horse and is sometimes called a trace or a tug. It runs from the hame attached to the collar around the neck of the horse beside the back legs to the single tree behind. A vigorous horse may in kicking get his leg on the outside of the strap giving rise to this saying.
"Feeling good enough to ...."

KICKS RIGHT OFF

Internal combustion engine in good tune and starts instantly.

KILL CULL

Terminally ill chicken. Euthanasia is the treatment for this condition. To cull is to go through any collection to throw out those not fit or suitable.

KILLED A BEAR

Made a good deal. It's a steal.
To purchase at or below cost.

KILL 'EM, COOK 'EM, AND EAT 'EM

Freshness is important in the preparation of wild game.
Result of a successful quail hunt.

KILL 'EM WITH KINDNESS

How to treat a very grouchy person.

KILLING TIME

Idle.
"You busy?" "Naw, just ...."

KILL OR CURE

Strong medicine.
"Here, take this. It will either ... you."

KILL TWO BIRDS WITH ONE STONE

Accomplish multiple tasks with one effort. Duplicitous results with singular activity.
When you give her a box of candy in hopes she will accept your request for a date, you also know chocolate is a mild aphrodisiac so you ....

KISS AMERICA

What you are doing when you slip on the ice and fall down face first anywhere in the United States.
As traction devices are attached to footwear you say, "I'll do anything to keep from having to ...."

KISSED ONE DOG AND IT DIED

Answer to: "Honey, give me a kiss."
Caution: You may end up in the doghouse when using this phrase.

KISSY FACE

The act of necking, smooching.
Usually preceded by the word, "Play ...."

KNEE DEEP IN CLOVER

Best of circumstances.
Relates to grazing animals with plenty to eat.

KNEE HIGH TO A GRASSHOPPER (JACKRABBIT) (DUCK)

Facetious comparative height description of a small child.
"I've known him since he was ...."

KNOCKED HIM COLD AS A WEDGE

Rendered unconscious by a blow to the head.

KNOCKED THE SALE

Disinterested party not involved in a trading deal points out a flaw which results in no sale. Usually relates to horse trading.

KNOCKED THE SUPREME HECK OUT OF

Practically destroyed. Very damaging. As in heavy frost damaging tender plants.
"It wasn't much of a fight—he ... him in one blow."

KNOCKED UP TURKEY

Overweight female.
"She gained so much weight that she looks like a ...."

KNOCK ON WOOD

For good luck ....

KNOW WHICH SIDE THEIR BREAD IS BUTTERED ON

With whom to curry favor. Lackey. Obsequious.

KNUCKLE BUSTER

An old worn out wrench likely to slip off the nut when pressure is applied resulting in an injury to the hand.

L

LADY-FINGER

A very small firecracker.

LADY LUCK

The gal you want on your side in any game.

LAID BY

The last time a farm row crop is cultivated during the growing season.

LAID OUT

Verbally attacked for an infraction. To scold.
Ready for burial.
Sunbather.
Female who did not come home all night and supposition is that sexual activity occurred.
Hen at the end of her laying cycle.

LAID UP

Sick in bed.

LAND OF GOSHEN!

A statement of amazement. Will wonders never cease.

LAST BUT NOT LEAST

Important topic or event comes up late on the agenda.

LAST OF THE MOHICANS

Used to refer to anything that is the last of a supply.
As in the final apple or potato removed from the cellar.

[THE] LAST STRAW

An act which provokes one to draw the line.
After a long streak of absurd actions retribution is imminent.

LAWS WERE MADE TO BE BROKEN

Contributing factor to the livelihood of attorneys.

LAWSY MERCY

I don't believe it or at least "I'm surprised."

LAY DRUNK

Intoxicated to the point of being horizontal.

LAYING FOR YOU

Waiting in concealment for opportunity to pounce.
Refers to the habit of a dog, whereby it will lie flat on the ground before attacking.
"After what you did to him, he'll be ...."

LAZY WHELP
Indolent child.

LEAD FOOT
Fast driver.

LEAD IN HIS BRITCHES
Laziness.

LEAD IN YOUR PENCIL
Virile. Increased sexual ability. Used jokingly among men.
Some say a strong alcoholic drink will put ....

LEAD POISONING
Shot with a firearm.
"If he comes through that door with robbery on his mind I'll give him a case of ... with my ol' thirty-eight."

LEAKING LIKE A SIEVE
Faulty liquid container or retainer.
"That bucket is ...."

LEAVE IT ALONE, MAYBE IT'LL GO AWAY
A thought as you ignore someone you don't like.

LEAVE NO STONE UNTURNED
A thorough investigation.

LEAVE NOTHING TO THE IMAGINATION
Totally nude.
Scanty clothing on a female.
Variation: Leave something to the imagination.

LEAVE THOSE FOR SEED
Not a thorough cleaning.
Objects left unmoved during a cleanup operation.

LED DOWN THE GARDEN PATH
Taken for a ride.
Deceived.

LEFT-HANDED MONKEY WRENCH

Sending a novice assistant to the toolbox for a tool which has no dextral direction.
"Hand me that ... out of the pickup."

LEGAL BEAGLES

Lawyers. Beagles are hunting dogs: Lawyers hunting fees rather than justice.

[THE] LESSER OF TWO EVILS

An undesirable choice.
In choosing between two political candidates, the choice is sometimes ....

LET 'ER FLICKER

Generally to let anything start.
Specifically to urinate (male), or turn on a water tap.

LET 'ER RIP

A command or permission to proceed.
Usually refers to the acceleration of an automobile.
Variation: "... potato chip!"

LET IT ALL HANG OUT

Tell it like it is. Bring forth all the facts. Reveal everything.

LET IT GLUE

Close the damper of the wood burning stove and let the embers slowly burn.

LET IT GO AT THAT

Leave a job not quite finished to your satisfaction.
Let an insult go by without a confrontation over it.

LET IT REST

Gossip rehashed too many times brings this remark to put an end to it.

LET'S GET IT DOWN IN WRITING

Culmination of a verbal contract.

LET'S GET THIS SHOW ON THE ROAD
Intent is to get activities started.
"Enough of this dilly dallying, ..."

LET SLEEPING DOGS LIE
Don't question or mention a bad situation that has gone on a long time.

LET'S MAKE THE CIRCLE
Said to a pet who accompanies you while doing the evening farm chores.

LET'S TAKE A QUICK LOOK-SEE
Short survey of the situation. Cursory examination.
To investigate suspicious activity.

LET THE CHIPS FALL WHERE THEY MAY
The action is over; results are forthcoming.
A word or deed is done—now you must bear the consequences.
"Go forward with your controversial plan and ...."

LET THEM STEW AWHILE
Allowing someone or a group to work out their frustrations themselves instead of getting involved yourself.

LETTING IT OUT
Expressing your complaints or disappointments, even though it doesn't do any good.

LET TOMORROW TAKE CARE OF ITSELF
Don't fret over an impending crisis.

LET YOUR DINNER SETTLE
Rest awhile before going back to work. Stay and visit awhile.

LICKED 'ER UP SLICK AND CLEAN
All food eaten and plate bare.

LIGHTNING NEVER STRIKES IN THE SAME PLACE TWICE
Rarely will a tragedy repeat itself in the same way and position geographically.
Also used for good or bad luck.

LIGHTNIN'S A-DANCIN'
Electrical activity preceding a thunderstorm.
"You kids get in here, ...!"

LIGHT ON HIS TOES
A good dancing partner.

LIKE A BULL IN A CHINA SHOP
Clumsy, negligent, uncoordinated, erratic, inattentive.
Destructive by accidental means.

LIKE A HEN TRYING TO HATCH A GOLF BALL
Impossible situation.

LIKE A HOUSE AFIRE
Fast moving.
"He's going at it ...."

LIKE A TORTOISE AT A SLOW TROT
Work progressing slowly.
Answer to, "How ya doing?" "I'm goin' ...."

LIKE NOBODY'S BUSINESS
Really going to town. Like it was going out of style. Fast.
Rapid accomplishment of a task.

LIKEN TO THAT
Similar to. Like that.

LIKE PULLIN' EYE TEETH
Difficult job. Collection of a debt from a laggard is ....

LIKE TALKING TO THE WALL
Giving very important advice to one who is not heeding it.

LIKE TO NEVER GOT OUT

After being stuck in the mud with a motor vehicle and the slow retrieval was finally successful.

LIKE THE BLIND LEADING THE BLIND

Two persons treading the same confused direction.
An inexpert advising an inexperienced.

LIKE THE DOG CHASING A CAR—HE WOULDN'T KNOW WHAT TO DO WITH IT IF HE CAUGHT IT

Used to identify with an elderly man seeking the hand of a much younger woman or anyone trying for a useless objective.

LIKE THE OLD LADY SAID WHEN SHE SPIT IN THE CHURN: "EVERY LITTLE BIT HELPS"

Small contributions do add up. Generally refers to things such as a light shower of rain, a small sale or gleanings from a sparse field of crops.

LIKE WALKING ON EGGS

A precarious situation.
"Negotiations were so precarious that it was ...."

LIMBER AS A RAG

Lithe as a well conditioned dancer.
Passed out, unconscious, limp.
Wilted, as a three-day-old vegetable.

LIMP ALONG

Adverse conditions cause slow progress of a project.
Also used as in the case of a motor vehicle barely moving under its own power.

LISTEN TO HER SNORT

Answer to a female tongue lashing.

LISTEN TO THE WIND BLOW

Answer to someone telling a falsehood or bragging excessively. Said in a sing song manner and usually repeated several times.

LIT INTO

To attack verbally or physically.
"When he came dragging in at 3 a.m., she ... him with a vengeance."

LIT OUT

Depart.
"Jake still here?" "No, he done ...."

LITTLE BUT MIGHTY

Short on stature but long on energy and motivation.

LITTLE BUTTERBEAN

Doting mother's term for a favorite child.
"How's my ... today?"

LITTLE FLY UPON THE WALL
AIN'T YOU GOT NO CLOTHES AT ALL
AIN'T YOU GOT NO PANTS OR SHIRT
AIN'T YOU GOT NO PETTISKIRT
AIN'T YOU COLD

Child's rhyme.

LITTLE HOT ROCK

A young virile male.

LITTLE PEOPLE TALK ABOUT PEOPLE
MEDIUM PEOPLE TALK ABOUT THINGS
BIG PEOPLE TALK ABOUT IDEAS

I have no idea what this means, because I am so busy talking about my possessions and discussing my neighbors' faults.

LITTLE PRAIRIE FLOWER

Petite, adorable, beautiful woman. Sometimes used with sarcasm to indicate a clinging vine type woman who is spoiled.
Sometimes said in baby talk: "Poor Wittle Pwairwe Fower," as a pronouncement of false sympathy.

LIT UP LIKE A CHRISTMAS TREE

Brightly illuminated.
A house at night with every light on.
A plane in flight at night.
"Joneses must be having a party tonight. Their house is ...."

LIVE AND LEARN

A lesson is learned through a mistake.

LIVE FAST, DIE YOUNG—LEAVE A GOOD LOOKING CORPSE

Excuse for excessive partying.

LIVE ONE

A solid sales prospect.

LIVE ON TO FIGHT ANOTHER DAY

Consolation for losing a fight or argument.
"We'll ...."

LIVING IN THE FAST LANE

Wringing all out of life there is. Utmost activity with regard to one's ability.

LOADED TO THE GILLS

Drunk.

LOADED TO THE HILT

Rich.

LOCKED UP TIGHTER THAN A JUG

Secure building.

LOCK 'EM UP

To incarcerate or put in the hoosegow.
Apply brakes on a motor vehicle with such force that all wheels cease to rotate and therefore slide with the resulting loss of steering direction.

LONG ABOUT DAYLIGHT

Early morning.
"... that ol' bobcat let out a terrible scream and the hogs scattered like flies escaping a barn swallow."

LONG AS YOUR ARM

Extensive listing.
"We have a waiting list for sweet corn as ...."

LONG DANGLES

Meritorious military service medals as opposed to campaign ribbons which are abbreviated medals. In the United States Navy they are worn at formal inspections.

LONG DRAWN OUT PROCESS (AFFAIR)

A task taking too long to complete. Unnecessary delay. As in government red tape.

[THE] LONGER I CHEWED IT, THE BIGGER IT GOT

A tough piece of meat brings this comment from the chewer.

LONG IN THE COUPLING POLE

Tall person.
Note: Coupling pole is the member that holds the front and back axles of some types of wagons together. It is sometimes adjustable as to length.

LONG LOST COUSIN

Friendly greeting to a person not seen in quite some time.
"I was greeted at the door like a ...."

LONG TALL SALLY

Slender female.

LONG TIME NO SEE

Greeting after a period of separation.

LOOK AT THE BRIGHT SIDE

Each and every dark cloud has a silver lining.

LOOK ME RIGHT SQUARE IN THE EYE
A request to repeat a statement you don't believe while you look for some clue to the authenticity in the reflexes of the eye. "... and repeat that story."

LOOKS GOOD ENOUGH TO EAT
Beautiful floral display.

LOOKS LIKE A COW SPIT BRAN IN YOUR FACE
Statement to a child with freckles.

LOOKS LIKE HE JUST CRAWLED OUT FROM UNDER HIS MOTHER'S WING
Young looking for the position he is in.
Not dry behind the ears yet.

LOOKS LIKE HE WOULD WISE UP
Said about a person who constantly makes matters worse for himself by repeatedly making the same mistakes in judgment.

LOOKS LIKE IT COULD CLABBER UP AND RAIN
Showers likely.
Thickening clouds compared to the thickening of milk as it curdles.

LOOKS LIKE SHE WAS POURED INTO THEM
Lady in tight fitting jeans.

LOOKS LIKE YOU COULD HAVE SIRED A GIRL, YOU HAD THE PATTERN RIGHT IN FRONT OF YOU
Said to the father of a newborn baby boy.

LOOKS LIVED IN
A comfortable home with informal decor. An excuse for not keeping house properly.

LOOKY LOOKY LOOKY, HERE COMES COOKY
Said to someone arriving overdressed for the occasion.

LOOP-LEGGED
Intoxicated.

LOOSE AS A COW'S TAIL
Barely attached causing excessive vibration of a part of a machine. Bolt on a machine in the process of becoming unfastened or loose. Flapping tin on the roof of a barn.

LOOSE AS A GOOSE
Generally refers to a person who doesn't tense up under pressure, or when his performance determines the outcome of an endeavor.

LOST IN THE SHUFFLE
Existing in the big city.

LOST YOUR SHIRT
Financial means depleted.
Generally refers to loss of financial reserves as the result of gambling.

LOVE MAKES THE WORLD GO ROUND, BUT MONEY GREASES THE WHEEL
True affection is often based upon the security of wealth.

LOVE MANY—TRUST FEW BUT ALWAYS PADDLE YOUR OWN CANOE
Be caring, wary and self reliant.
A saying popular in the 1930s as an entry in grade school autograph book.

LUCK OF THE IRISH
Good fortune befalls you and this comment results.

M

MADE ME SO MAD I COULDN'T SEE STRAIGHT
Intense frustration, irritation, anger.

MADE MY BLOOD RUN COLD
Shocking, fearful experience. Result of viewing a serious accident scene.

MADE OUT LIKE A BANDIT
Good fortune while pursuing an enterprise.
To score with a female.

MADMAN MUNTZ
One who acts or drives as if crazy.

MAIN STRENGTH AND AWKWARDNESS
Manpower makes up for lack of aptitude.
Got the job done but not in the most optimum manner.
Clumsy approach to a project.
"How on earth did you get that buggy up on the barn roof?"
"...."

MAKE A FEDERAL CASE OUT OF IT
Big to-do about nothing.
"All I got was a traffic ticket and you ...."

MAKE HAY WHILE THE SUN SHINES—MAKE HASTE WHEN IT RAINS
Do the job at the most opportune time.
Take advantage of an opportunity before it passes.

MAKE IT SNAPPY—I AIN'T GOT ALL DAY
Hurry up. I command you to move quickly.
Right now.

MAKES MY BOTTOM HURT
Empathy.

MAKES NO BONES ABOUT IT

Unabashed and vocal about a subject.
Brings it out in the open.

MAKES ME NO NEVER-MIND

It makes no difference to me.

MAKE THE FUR FLY

Intense activity.
"We don't stir around in the morning very early, but when we do we ...."

MAN, HAVE WE EVER GOT THEM

An abundance of goods for sale.

MAN, I RECKON

That sure is the truth. I agree with you.

MANY HANDS MAKE LIGHT WORK

Let's all pitch in and finish the job so no one of us will be overly tired when the task is finished.

MARRIED RIGHT OUT OF THE CRADLE

Young bride.

MAYBE IT WILL SLACK OFF A LITTLE

Waiting for a shower to end so work can be resumed.

MAYBE SO, MAYBE NO

Substantiate your statement with facts.
There is a possibility that what you say is the truth, but I doubt it.

MEAL TICKET

The skill or assignment that guarantees continuation in a job.

MEAN MOTOR SCOOTER AND A BAD GO-GETTER

One who dresses stylishly and cavorts with abandon.

MEANWHILE BACK AT THE RANCH

Usually used to indicate things going normally at home. A phrase used frequently in early western serials.

MEEK AS A LAMB

Usually describing reaction to orders or criticism.

MEET YOURSELF COMING AND A-GOING

Very busy at a job where one travels to and fro.

MELLOWS WITH AGE

Comparing a gracefully aging person to good whiskey.

ME, MYSELF AND I

Have taken sole responsibility.
"Who is responsible for this mess?" "...."

ME OWING YOU MONEY IS BETTER THAN HAVING IT IN THE BANK

You can withdraw it from the bank and spend it foolishly, but you can't get it out of me.

MERCY SAKES!

Amazement, shock, consternation, dismay.

MESS WITH THE BULL YOU GET THE HORN

Beware, you may get more than you bargained for.

MIGHT AS WELL BE USEFUL AS ORNAMENTAL

Putting someone to work who was just standing around observing.

MIGHT AS WELL EAT THE END OFF A FENCE POST

A comparison of the nutritional value and texture of a store-bought tomato versus a homegrown variety or any store-bought vegetable.

MIGHT NIGH

Almost. Near miss.
Actually means mighty near.

"As I hurried down the path I stepped on the tail of a crossing copperhead and he ... bit me."

MILKIN' THE KITTY

Taking money from the cash drawer for personal use.

MILK IT DRY

Rending every last bit of profit from a venture.

MILK THE TOURISTS

Selling to or serving tourists.

MIND YOUR MANNERS

Admonition to a child leaving for a visit to the home of another without parental supervision.
"... and don't lick your knife."

MISERY LOVES COMPANY

Association with others who share a common misfortune is often good therapy.

MISSED A LICK

In the pursuance of an endeavor one stumbles but recovers and picks up the beat.

MISS PRISS

A fastidious, reserved, queenly, aloof woman.
Derogatory remark about a woman who thinks she is hot stuff.
"Who does ... think she is?"

[THE] MOMENT OF TRUTH

All facts come to light. As in cutting a watermelon when there is a question as to its ripeness.

MONEY-HUNGRY FOOL

Overly obsessed with the desire to acquire large amounts of financial resources, and doesn't care how it is done.

MONEY ISN'T EVERYTHING

A vocation purely for monetary gain is not always best.
You can't buy happiness or health.
Variation: "... but it beats the heck out of whatever is in second place."

MONEY-MAD

Excessively preoccupied with the pursuit of financial resources.

MONEY TALKS

A monetary offer will hurry the deal.

MONKEY ON A STRING

Henpecked husband.
Dances to the employer's tune.
Entirely under the influence of another.
"She leads him around just like a ...."

MONKEY SEE MONKEY DO

Copycat. Keeping up with the Joneses.

MORE FUN THAN A BARREL OF MONKEYS

Someone pleasant to be around.
Comical activity.

MORE THAN I CAN SAY GRACE OVER

Overextended. Grace in this case is a prayer to God for help in getting a job done.

MORE THAN MEETS THE EYE

All facts not revealed. Tip of the iceberg. Likelihood that important underlying issues are present.

MORE THAN ONE WAY TO SKIN A CAT

Elusive goal calls for different tactics. Different solutions to the same problem.
If an avenue becomes blocked there are others.

[THE] MORE THE MERRIER
Pleasure enhanced by increased numbers at a festive gathering.
[One of the sadder opposite true stories I've heard was about a fellow who had a "kegger" at his house on his birthday and no one showed up.]

MORTGAGE LIFTERS
Hogs raised for sale.

MOTHER-IN-LAW SEAT
Rear seating in an automobile.

MOTOR-MOUTH
A talkative person.

MOVE OVER, SMALL DOG, TALL DOG MOVING IN
Pronouncement of dominance. Used by persons while involved in the process of mate selection.

MOVING UPSTAIRS LIKE A HOMESICK ANGEL
Rapidly climbing aircraft.

MUCKELTY COLORED
Generally used to denote hair coat color on an animal which has many colors, shades and hues.
Used primarily with reference to calico cats.

MUD-IN OATS; DUST-IN WHEAT
Used as advice to a newcomer who is farming for the first time. Moisture conditions of the soil at planting time for these two crops make it practical to sow seed in less than optimum soil conditions. In this part of the country oats are sown in early spring when soils are generally damp. Wheat is planted in the fall when soils are generally dryer.

MUNGY LOOKING
Dirty in appearance.

MY ACHING BACK

Don't tell me your troubles, I've got them of my own.
Trouble on the way.
"Oh ..., here comes the bill collector."

MY BETTER HALF

Affectionate description for wife.

MY BUTT IS DRAGGING SO LOW IT IS COVERING MY TRACKS

Very tired after working hard all day.

MY CLAVICLE

Balderdash.
Do you expect me to believe that preposterous story?
"City water is more pure than well water." "...!"

MY FEEL BAD HURTS

As in the case of a headache and a stomach ache at the same time.

MY FOOT!

A statement of reverse appraisal.
"Me pay you? ..., you owe my money."

MY GET UP AND GO DONE GOT UP AND WENT

Tired, listless.

MY HOW TIME FLIES WHEN YOU'RE HAVING FUN

Jokingly used when involved in drudgery.

MY LANDS A-LIVIN'!

Isn't that amazing? Whatever got into him to cause such action? Would you believe?

MY LITTLE OLD BEAN

Self derision as to the capability of one's repository of intelligence.

MY MOMMA DIDN'T RAISE NO FOOL

Egotistical self-appraisal.

MY MOTHER, WHILE CARRYING ME IN HER WOMB, LISTENED TO A BROKEN RECORD BUT IT DIDN'T AFFECT ME—DIDN'T AFFECT ME—DIDN'T AFFECT ME

Child's saying of the 1930s.

MY MOUTH TASTES LIKE THE RUSSIAN ARMY WALKED THROUGH IT BAREFOOTED

Assessment of one's condition the morning after a night of excessive partying and consumption of alcoholic beverages.

N

NAME YOUR POISON

Asking a person what he wants to drink.

NATURAL BORN LIAR

Habitual prevaricator.

NATURE OF THE BRUTE (BEAST)

Method of operation. What may be idiosyncratic to you is only natural behavior for another.
A machine that consistently operates in an erratic manner.
"Why does that old tractor of yours steer so hard?"
"That's just the ...."

NECESSITIES, NEEDS, AND WANTS

Prioritizing meager resources.
[I once had a farm loan banker who required me to assign priorities to my requests for funds in these categories. Since the fellow was a good banker, it is needless to say, he loaned money only for the necessities.]

NEEDS A NEW FLINT

Said when an automobile engine will not start.
Relates to a pocket cigarette lighter with sparking device absent and it will not light, or to a flintlock rifle.

NERVOUS AS A CAT

Agitated mental state.
As in the case of a father awaiting the birth of his first offspring.

NEST OF THIEVES

A bad store or tavern.

NEVER A DULL MOMENT

Atmosphere of an active household with many children.

NEVER CAN TELL

The answer to a question where outcome is uncertain.
"You think it will rain?" "You ...."

NEVER (TO) DARKEN THEIR DOOR AGAIN

Will not ever return.
"The way they treated me, I will ...."

NEVER LAID A HAND ON HER

Answer to accusation of sexual encounter with female.

NEVER LET THE SUN GO DOWN ON A DEBT

Conservative admonition.
This was actively preached and practiced in rural areas of America in the past.

NEVER MISSED A LICK

Admiration for a steady hard worker.
Long hours of hard work without fail.
"That old truck and I just traveled a thousand miles and she ...."

**NEVER RUN WHEN YOU CAN WALK
NEVER WALK WHEN YOU CAN SIT
NEVER SIT WHEN YOU CAN LIE DOWN**

Admonishment to a workaholic.

NEVER TEASE AN OLD DOG, HE MIGHT HAVE ONE BITE LEFT

Advanced age does not necessarily mean a lack of ability or motivation to answer a challenge.
[My father, while in his early eighties, ran off two punks who were taunting him in front of the poolhall. He drew back his fist and advanced while releasing a stream of expletives. A poolhall full of WWI veteran cronies would have come to his aid if needed.]

NEVER TRUST ANYONE WHO DOESN'T FISH AND DRINK ALCOHOL

A fellow fisherman's favorite saying.

NEVER UNDERESTIMATE THE POWER OF A WOMAN

Females have vast resources of fortitude, courage, craftiness, patience, connivance, intelligence, aptitude, vision, intuition and sexuality. They do not hesitate to use them all in their conduct of relations with men. On top of that, they on average live longer than men so end up controlling most of the money and thereby more power.

NEW DEAL WEED

A weed that first started showing up in the crop fields of the Ozarks during the first term of President Franklin D. Roosevelt (1932). Sometimes called white top.

NEW LEASE ON LIFE

Starting over after a calamity.
Release from the hospital after a serious illness gives one a feeling of having a ....

NICE AS PIE

One who is very obliging.

NICE-LOOKING PIECE OF HORSE FLESH

Beautiful equine specimen.
This is considered a nice compliment if you are the owner of the horse.

NICE, PEACEABLE FOLK

Appraisal of good, friendly, quiet neighbors.

NICE TO MAKE YOUR ACQUAINTANCE

Said to a person you have just met. Similar to, but a bit more formal than, "pleased to meet you."

NICE WEATHER FOR DUCKS

Rainy period and the speaker, not being a duck, is not too thrilled with the gloomy atmospheric conditions.

NICKEL AND DIME YOU TO DEATH

Many small repairs to a motor vehicle add up to a tidy sum over a period of time.

NICKEL NURSE

Drink alcoholic beverages very slowly at a bar.
To slowly sip one's drink.
Opposite of "chugalug."

NICKEL'S WORTH OF FIVE DOLLAR BILLS

Imaginary amount. Said by one who may have needs but not the money to pay.
"I am going to town; do you need anything?"
"Yeah, a ...."

[THE] NIGHT YOU SLEEP NAKED

Facetious description of Saturday night.

NINETY NINE BOTTLES OF BEER ON THE WALL
NINETY NINE BOTTLES OF BEER
IF ONE OF THOSE BOTTLES SHOULD HAPPEN TO FALL
NINETY EIGHT BOTTLES OF BEER ON THE WALL

A singsong verse sang on long trips in the 1940s.
Repeat until reaching one bottle of beer on the wall.
Start over with ninety nine bottles of beer on the wall if the trip is long enough and vocal cords hold out.
Variation: Ninety nine blue bottles a-hanging on the wall.

NINETY TO NOTHING

Fast travel by automobile.

"Here he comes in that old flivver going ...."

NO BIG DEAL

Insignificant.

"Thank you so much for your help." "...."

NO BIGGER THAN A MINUTE

Newborn babes.

NOBODY IN HIS RIGHT MIND WOULD

A distasteful task is prefaced by this statement.

"... grow okra if he had to pick it."

NO FOOLING?

Are you telling me the truth?

NO FOOL LIKE AN OLD FOOL

Actions unbecoming an elderly person. Usually refers to an older man frolicking with a younger woman, the net result being to her advantage.

NO LIE

This is said as a question after someone tells you something lacking authenticity.

"Janet said she would go out with me." "...?"

NO LOVE LOST BETWEEN THOSE TWO

Dislike by mutual agreement.

NO MAD RUSH

Take your time.

[THE] NON-DRINKER'S CURSE

Getting up in the morning feeling as good as you will all day.

NONE OF YOUR BEESWAX

It's my own business what I do.

NO NEWS IS GOOD NEWS

Worry not until the facts are known.

One who frets over a late arrival is soothed by saying ....

NO QUESTIONS ASKED

A free hand. Do what you want.

Return of a missing item with impunity.

NO REMARKS FROM THE PEANUT GALLERY

Your comments are neither solicited nor welcome.

When theaters had three galleries or levels, the top was the cheapest—peanuts = small amount.

NO REST FOR THE WICKED

Long hours of toil await those devoid of morals.

NORMAL RED-BLOODED AMERICAN BOY

Average young U.S. male.

"Why do you go out night after night chasing women?" "I'm just a ...."

NOSE OUT OF JOINT

Unnecessary jealousy. Perturbed for no reason. Envious beyond reason. One who reacts negatively to a slight is said to have his ....

NOT A BIT WELL

Sick person getting much worse.

NOT A DRY THREAD ON HIM

Result of being caught out in a sudden rain storm without protection.

NOT A HAIR OUT OF PLACE

Elegantly dressed and immaculately coiffured.

NOT AN OUNCE OF FAT

A thin person.

An efficient operation.

NOT A WORRY IN THE WORLD
Oblivious to tumultuous surroundings. Ability to avoid concern.

NOT BAD MANNERS, JUST GOOD BEER
When an unsuppressed belch occurs this statement often follows.

NOT DRY BEHIND THE EARS
Very immature adult.

NO TELLING WHERE
Someone or something is missing. Whereabouts unknown.

NOT ENOUGH HORSEPOWER TO WIPE YOUR NOSE
Aircraft with a small engine power plant compared to the overall size and weight.

NOT ENOUGH TO SETTLE THE DUST
Answer to the question as to the amount of precipitation. "How much rain did you get?" "...."

NOT ENOUGH TO STUFF IN YOUR EYEBALL
A very small amount. Poor production. Light crop yields. Business way off.
"Are you getting very many tomatoes from your garden now?" "...."

NOT FIT FOR MAN NOR BEAST
Intolerable weather conditions.

NOTHING VENTURED, NOTHING GAINED
Failure is certain for those who do not even try.
Pursuing a goal where the outcome is in doubt, but the prospects for success justify the risks.
Risk bearing for profit.

NOT HOLDING YOUR MOUTH RIGHT
Something done the same way works for others but not for you. "I can't get the lid off of this catsup bottle." "You are ...."

'NOT I,' SAID THE LITTLE RED HEN
Proclamation of innocence.

NOT LONG ON MODESTY, IS HE?
Used to describe the male of a pair cavorting sexually in public view such as a rooster and hen or stallion and mare.

NOT OUT OF THE WOODS YET
Trial and tribulation will continue. The debt is yet to be paid. Making headway but the ordeal is far from over.

NOT QUITE RIPE YET
Water in ice cube trays not frozen solid.

NOT SO FAST
Catching someone in the act of appropriating your property.
"... young man, those are my shoes you are wearing."
Also widely used in logical discussion.

NOT TICKING ON ALL OF THEM
A person not using all his mental ability.
"Them" = cylinders of an internal combustion engine.

NOT WHAT IT'S CRACKED UP TO BE
Disputing a highly touted theory. Things are not always as they seem. Reading the fine print in a guarantee. Highly touted venture becomes a failure. Does not live up to expectation. Disappointing performance.

NOT WORTH A PLUG NICKEL
Something of little value.
Sometimes used to describe a lazy person.

NO UNCERTAIN TERMS
Clear proclamation. Definite, clear statement.
"I told him in ... to watch his step when he is in the presence of my girlfriend."

NO WAY, JOSE
Will not go along with you.

NOW I KNOW

Used when an action or event makes clear why an earlier event or action had happened.
Information long sought finally becomes available.
"After a visit to the doctor to see why she could not keep her breakfast down, it was determined that she is pregnant. ...."

NOW IS THE TIME FOR ALL GOOD MEN TO COME TO THE AID OF THEIR PARTY (COUNTRY)

A warm-up sentence used in typing class which causes the fingers to move across the keyboard extensively.

NOW OR NEVER

Immediate action necessary or opportunity will not present itself again.
"I have asked for your hand in marriage three times. The time has come for an answer. It is ...."

NOW WE'RE COOKING

Things going well after a period of adversity.

NOW WHAT?

After a series of mishaps another becomes apparent.

NOW YOU'RE TALKING

I agree with what you say.

NUBBIN BUSTER

Extensive, slow, soaking rain.
Nubbin is the second ear on a cornstalk, usually small.

'NUFF SAID

End of conversation.

NUMBER IS UP

Death imminent.
"When the bullet with your name on it arrives, your ...."

NUTS AND BOLTS

Down to the basics of a business venture. Financing arranged, building acquired and merchandise arranged on the shelves would be called the ... of the enterprise.

NUTTIER THAN A FRUITCAKE

Behavior denotes similarity to that of an idiot. Silly actions unbecoming to a sane person.

Mostly used in a jocular vein about a friend who is actually witty and fun to be around.

NUT WARD

Hospital quarters for the mentally deficient.

O

OFF THE DEEP END

Head over heels in love.

Overly charged up in the carrying out of one's duties.

Zealous to the point of being ridiculous.

Unconventional behavior.

"He is sixty; she is thirty; he has gone ...."

OFF THE WALL REMARK

Speaking without the aid of notes or research.

OFF TO A ROUSING START

Used in the negative sense to denote a slow beginning.

Business slow or nonexistent at the beginning of the day.

OFF TO A RUNNING START

Quick departure.

"We were in the fields before daylight and ...."

OLD AS THE HILLS

Aged person, structure, or tale.

As in reference to an ancient term, phrase or joke.

OLD CROAT (COOT)
Elderly person.
Usually refers to a man.

OLDER BUT WISER
Learning from an unfortunate circumstance of the past.

OLD HULDY
Beloved aged truck.

OLD MAIDS
Unpopped kernels at the bottom of a bowl of popcorn.
A card game called Old Maids; also used (singular) in reference to the Queen of Spades in the card game "Hearts."

OLD MAN WINTER
Season of cold temperatures, wind, and snow.
Don't let his age fool you, he can still be ferocious.
"Fetch in the wood, ... is fast upon us."

OLD MAN WINTER KINDA SLIPPED UP ON US
Real cold day after a warm fall season.

OLD SNEAKNOSE
The one animal in a group who is always looking for a way out of an enclosure.

OLD STOMPIN' GROUND
A place of former residence or activity.
Return to a former habitat is a visit to the ....

OLD STUT AND SPUTTER
A person with a speech impediment.

[THE] OLD WAR-HORSE
Wife of henpecked husband and always battle ready.
Battle-ax. Tempestuous woman.

ONCE BURNT, TWICE CAUTIOUS
A disastrous mistake in judgment tends to make one more careful under similar circumstances in the future.

An unwed mother who is now on the pill and not dating men is said to be ....

ONE FOOT IN THE GRAVE

Near death.
Variation: ... and the other on a banana peel.

**ONE FOR THE MONEY
TWO FOR THE SHOW
THREE TO GET READY AND
FOUR TO GO**

Chant of a person starting a race. The race starts with the word "go."

ONE-LINER

A joke or humorous saying consisting of only one sentence.

ONE MAN'S TRASH, ANOTHER MAN'S TREASURE

There are a lot of antiques around that came from a junk pile.

ONE MORE STAR IN YOUR CROWN

As in the case of a bedside vigil (for the death) of a friend or relative.

ONE OF THESE DAYS

After a series of annoyances, one announces in this way that the source of the irritation is going to be eliminated.
Used as a phrase of procrastination for any unspecified future time.
"... I'll get that leak fixed."

ONE STEP AHEAD OF THE LAW

On the run with officials in hot pursuit.

ONE STEP AT A TIME

Proceed in a deliberate and orderly manner.

[THE] ONE THAT GOT AWAY

The biggest fish.

[THE] ONE WE BEEN LOOKING FOR

The last of any repetitive chore. End of a long hard job of piecework. The last ear of corn picked from a large field or debeaking the last chicken in a flock.

ONE WOULD THINK HE'D KNOW BETTER

Behavior unbecoming a person's mental or intellectual capacities.

[THE] ONLY DIFFERENCE BETWEEN MEN AND BOYS IS THE SIZE OF THEIR TOYS

Males never grow up. Bicycles become motorcycles as go carts become hot rods.

[THE] ONLY FIGHT I EVER LOST WAS WHEN I SLIPPED WHILE RUNNING AROUND A CORNER

Evasive action wins fights. (Facetious.)

[THE] ONLY PEBBLE UPON THE BEACH

Comparing a person to a beach with only one stone showing to one with money.
"If he were ... he could have all the inheritance."
Or in the case of deflating an egoist: "She thinks she is ...."

[THE] ONLY THING I HAVE TO DO IS DIE

I will not grant your request.
"You have to get the income tax papers in the mail by April 15." "...."

ON THE JUG

Consumption of alcoholic beverages. As in the case of a person having a drinking problem and has repeatedly tried to quit and is referred to as ... again.

ON THE MONEY

Exactly right. Paying with the correct change.
Dead center. As in splitting a piece of firewood and hitting it in exact center.

OOPSIE DAISY

My mistake. Sorry about that. Apology. Surprise.
"... I spilled the milk."
Note: Not to be confused with "Upsy Daisy" which has an entirely different meaning.

OPEN MOUTH, INSERT FOOT, CHEW VIGOROUSLY

A modification of, "putting one's foot in one's mouth." Used to describe a faux pas.

OPEN UP A CAN OF WORMS

Any investigation that will lead to other infractions more significant.

OPERATING ON A SHOESTRING

With little resources or financial backing.

OPPORTUNITY ONLY KNOCKS ONCE

Watch and listen carefully for that moment when your calling is announced.
Sometimes it is very subtle indeed.

ORCHIDS AND ONIONS BOARD

Compliments or brickbats. Praise or complaints.
[A phrase related to me by an airline stewardess on a flight from San Francisco to Los Angeles in 1966, describing the bulletin board in their quarters where letters from customers are displayed denoting exceptionally good or bad services.]

OUGHT TO HAVE HIS (MY) HEAD EXAMINED

After making a serious mistake in judgment. This is said to oneself or about someone else.

OUNCE OF PREVENTION IS WORTH A POUND OF CURE

Maintenance pays off big.
Conscious effort to avoid calamity.

OUR EGGS ARE SO FRESH THE HENS HAVEN'T EVEN MISSED THEM YET

Newly laid eggs sold immediately.

OUT AND ABOUT

Away on business, pleasure or errands.

OUT IN FORCE

Large grouping on the move.
On major holidays the tourists and the police are ....

OUT OF POCKET

Not in one's proper place.
A person on vacation is described by fellow workers as being ... this week.
Also means costs that are paid in immediate cash.

OUT OF SIGHT, OUT OF MIND

Stay near the one you love.
One tends to forget those things not seen regularly.
The opposite of: "Absence makes the heart grow fonder."

OUT OF THE NOTION

A change of mind or desire.
Usually used with regard to a change in plans for a sexual encounter. "After the candle light dimmed and the red wine was poured, we retired to the fireside hearth; but she was ... by then."

OVER MY DEAD BODY

A stern caution as to how dedicated one is to his position.
"The only way you will proceed is ...."

OZARKS' DIAMONDS

Rocks which dot the landscape in hill country.
[This term was used by a friend after observing our front yard strewn with limestone boulders scattered by a construction blasting crew preparing the site for an underground Bell Telephone conduit.]

P

PACK IT IN
To quit work. Knock off for the day.

PAID MY DUES
Put in my time. Did my share. As in time served in the military defense of the country.

PALE AS A GHOST
Extreme case of fright.

PALM OF MY HAND
Well acquainted with a certain area.
"After traveling the state of Missouri for many years, I know it like the ...."

PAPER-SHUFFLER
Secretaries, accountants, lawyers or any person who handles written documents in the course of their work.

PAR FOR THE COURSE
Routine outcome. Perfect as usual.

PARTING SHOT
Last statement of a verbal exchange.

PATCH IT UP—FIX IT UP—WEAR IT OUT = MAKE IT DO
Conservative approach to care of a machine, clothing or appliance for extended life span.

PEA BRAIN
One of little intelligence.

PECKER-WOOD
Dumbhead. I don't like your actions.
"You ..., stay out of my beer."

PEEL YOUR HEAD

Threat of violence if you do not change your ways.
"I'll ... if you don't quit playing that silly guitar."

PEG IT

Driving an automobile as fast as the speedometer registers. Reference is that speed indicator needle actually touches a peg at the upper speed limit of the speedometer.

PENNY SAVED IS A PENNY EARNED

Thrift, even in small ways, is a virtue and will add up to a bundle over the years.

PEOPLE WHO LIVE IN GLASS HOUSES SHOULDN'T THROW STONES

Examine your own lifestyle before being critical of another's.
Derogatory remarks may boomerang.
Criticism may come back home to rest.

PERFECT FOOL

Person with little sense of direction or purpose in life.

PERK UP

To pay attention after having not done so.

PERSONALITY OF A SACK OF NAILS

One who lacks the basic social skills of wit, humor, conviviality, charm and grace.
The way one would describe his ex-wife's boyfriend.

PETE AND REPETE

Two people who hang around together a lot.

PH.D. DEGREE—ONE WHO GETS TO KNOW MORE AND MORE ABOUT LESS AND LESS UNTIL HE KNOWS EVERYTHING ABOUT NOTHING

Poking fun at the intellectual establishment.

PICKIN' AND A-GRINNIN'

Vegetable harvest in full swing with bountiful, profitable crop. Guitar musicians playing and enjoying themselves.

PICKIN' 'EM UP AND LAYIN' 'EM DOWN
Rapid movement on foot. Making tracks.
"After the first shot he was seen ... in retreat."

PICKIN' UP STEAM
Gradually accelerating. Business getting better.

PICK ME UP
Drink of any kind used to renew energy.

PICK OF THE LITTER
First choice of animal siblings with the same birth date. Also used jokingly in the evaluation of children of the same family.

PICK UP A FEW EXTRA SHEKELS
Income on the side over and above regular pay.
Moonlighters ... for their effort.
Shekel is a Hebrew unit of weight or a coin of that weight.

PICK UP THE PIECES
Start over. Resume normal activity after a disastrous event.
"After the funeral, we began to ...."

PIECE OF CAKE
Easily performed task for one who is trained.

PIG OUT
To overeat at a gathering.

PINCH BUTT
A person with a slender build.

[A] PINT'S A POUND THE WORLD AROUND
One way to remember the weight of 1/2 quart liquid or 16 ounces avoirdupois or anything that can be measured by liquid measure, like sugar.

PITCHER PUMP
A small hand operated pumping device for drawing water out of a cistern directly into the house.

[An improvement over the rain barrel. Ladies used the soft rainwater to wash their hair and do laundry. Due to its low mineral content, menfolk replenished auto battery liquid with the same water. Well water was used for drinking and cooking.]
Cistern: underground tank for storing rain water which has run off the roof of a structure.

PITIFUL PEARL
Unappealing, disheveled appearance of a woman.

PLACE TO HANG YOUR HAT
Home away from home.

PLAGG TAKE IT
Used in place of darn, dang or heck.
"..., can't you do anything right?"
Actually a mispronunciation of "plague."

PLAIN AS DAY
Obvious.

PLAYED RIGHT INTO MY HAND
One who unknowingly does what is best for your plans.

PLAYING CRINKLE FENDER
Driving erratically and apt to have a collision causing damage to the exterior of the automobile.

PLAYING FOR BLOOD
A game of cards where money is involved and absolutely no compassion or mercy is extended under any circumstances. No holds barred.

PLAYING FREEZE OUT
Driving an automobile with the window down or leaving the door to the house open on a cold day.

PLAYING IN THE DIRT
Tilling the soil preparatory to planting.
[Wife Kathryn's verbal reaction to my sometimes futile farming efforts.]

PLAY IT CLOSE TO YOUR VEST
Proceed with caution.
"Ulterior motives abound, so ...." Refers to the tactic in card playing whereby one holds the cards in such a manner as to discourage peeking by a bystander or another player.

PLAY SUCK FACE
Kissing.

PLAY TIP UP
To drink fast. A variation of chugalug.
Not recommended to be played with alcoholic beverages.

PLAY YOUR CARDS RIGHT
Can pull it off with proper strategy.
"If you ..., you can get her to go to the prom with you."

PLEASED TO MEET YOU
Your answer after being introduced to a person for the first time.
After a short conversation the parting statement to follow this phrase is: "Nice to have met you."

PLEASINGLY PLUMP
Condolatory flattery about a slightly obese person.

[THE] PLOT THICKENS
More information brings to light devious doings.
There is more than meets the eye.

POLITE COMPANY
Formal gathering.

POOL HALL, STUDY HALL, AND ALCOHOL
Three favorite subjects in college.

POOR AS JOB'S TURKEY
Small financial resources. Sad financial condition.

POOR BABY
Fake sympathy. Said to an adult who is acting childish and wanting unwarranted sympathy.
"My new Cadillac won't start!" "...."

[A] POOR EXCUSE IS BETTER THAN NONE
No matter how feeble, at least it's a try.

POP IT TO HER
Accelerate an automobile rapidly.

POPPIN' JOHNNY
Two cylinder John Deere tractor.

POP THE CORK
Let the party begin. Refers to the opening of a champagne bottle.

POSSESSION IS NINE TENTHS OF OWNERSHIP
A loaned tool becomes the property of another, given enough time for the original owner to forget where it went. Variation: Possession is nine tenths of the law.

POTATO BUG
A potbellied mandolin with alternating dark and light strips of wood on the backside of the sound chamber making it resemble the appearance of the adult Colorado Potato Beetle.

POTATOES WITH THE JACKETS ON
Spuds boiled with the peeling intact. Small new potatoes are usually cooked this way.
"What's for dinner? ..., fried chicken and new June peas."

POT'S RIGHT
Actually means all antes or bets are in the pot when playing poker.

Used in any situation where the count is correct.
"After exchanging a ten dollar bill for two fives, the ...."

POURED HIM ON THE BUS (PLANE, TRAIN)
After a period of drinking alcoholic beverages, an intoxicated friend is helped aboard a public conveyance to depart on a journey.
"I ... much to the chagrin of the attendants."

POUR ON THE COAL
To accelerate rapidly.

POWER IN THE BLOOD
A feeling of strength or invincibility.

POWERS THAT BE
Established authorities; sometimes people with determining control of the establishment.

PRANCIN' OR DANCIN'
A question of one's activity format.
Inept ballroom style leads one to remark, "Is he ...?"

PREGNANT ROLLER SKATE
Volkswagen Beetle automobile.

PREPARE TO MEET YOUR MAKER
Anybody about to die, or starting an undertaking that might result in death.
Said before euthanasia of a terminally ill farm animal.

PRETTIEST LITTLE THING I EVER LAID EYES ON
Observation with regard to a thing of beauty. Some examples are a beautiful girl, baby, colt or car.

PRETTY AS A PICTURE
Usually used to describe a beautiful young girl.

[THE] PRICE OF POKER IS GOING UP
New way of doing things that makes it cost more.
A new high stakes player entering an ongoing game of chance.

PRISON PALLOR
Pale complexion.

PRIVILEGED CHARACTER
One who enjoys special treatment such as a cat sleeping undisturbed on a busy doorstep.

[A] PRIVILEGE TALKING TO YOU
Respectful conclusion to a conversation.

PROMISE YOU THE MOON
Unscrupulous sales persons touting their product to the extreme. Amorous suitor in the spirit of the chase will sometimes ....

PROUD AS A JUNEBUG
Pleased with one's own appearance or accomplishments.

PRUNES, ORANGES, AND ALFALFA
Three kinds of kisses. Refers to lip position.

PTOMAINE PALACE
Poor quality eating establishment.

PULL THE PLUG
Divulge information damaging to another.

PULL THROUGH
Recover from a severe illness.

PULL UP ROOTS
A change in domicile location.

PULPIT POUNDER
Overzealous pastor. Advocate of the hell fire and brimstone approach to preaching.

PURE AS THE DRIVEN SNOW
Chaste. Completely honest.

PURE CORN
A stage act using ancient jokes of a mundane nature. Mawkish country style humor. Obsolete jokes or statements. Sometimes used to describe bourbon or whiskey.

PURPLE SHAFT
Unfair treatment in the eyes of the recipient.

PURRING LIKE A KITTEN
Engine running smoothly.

PUSH WATER
Gasoline or diesel automotive fuel.

PUT A BUG IN HIS EAR
Plant an idea in someone's head so they will carry out your wishes unknowingly. Put someone wise to the situation.

PUT A NICKEL IN IT
Said to a person whose automobile engine is being cranked but will not start. Connotation is to pay for the repairs and it will run. Originated at a time when a juke box required a nickel to make the music play.
Variation: Put a nickel in it and let the buffalo pull it. (Back when a nickel had a buffalo depicted on one side of the coin.)

PUT ANOTHER CUP OF WATER IN THE SOUP
Unexpected arrivals at mealtime calls for innovative strategy. The same idea as "Hamburger Helper," only cheaper.
"Company's a comin', ..."

PUT 'EM ALL IN A BAG—SHAKE 'EM UP—ROLL 'EM OUT ONE AT A TIME AND YOU COULDN'T TELL 'EM APART
A family or group of scoundrels where one is just as bad as the other.

PUT 'ER THERE
To shake hands as in the closing of a business deal. Sometimes used to indicate "I agree with you."

PUT IT OUT OF ITS MISERY
Euthanasia for a terminally ill animal.
In the case of a chicken it is referred to as stretching its neck.

PUT IT TO HIM
Attack vigorously; punish harshly or seek approval.

PUT ON YOUR HIKING BOOTS
Let's go. Said prior to departure on foot.

PUT OUT THE CLOCK AND WIND THE CAT
Bedtime. Used in times past when cats slept in the barn and clocks were not electric. [An elaborate spoonerism.]

PUT THAT IN YOUR PIPE AND SMOKE IT
Here are the facts—take it or leave it. This set of circumstances is not to your liking, but you will have to live with it.
"My assessment of your idea is that it stinks; ...."

PUTTING OUT THE FIRE
Handling a crisis at once. Borrowing money to pay off past due debts.

PUT UP OR SHUT UP
Make your bet or be quiet. Act or quit criticizing.

PUT YOUR (MY) FACE ON
Female applying makeup.

PUT YOUR MONEY WHERE YOUR MOUTH IS
Back up difference of opinion by offer to bet financial reserves on the outcome.

Q

QUEER AS A THREE DOLLAR BILL
Strange acting individual.

QUEER LOOKIN' DUCK, AIN'T HE?
Person with odd facial features. Person with habits of dress widely divergent from yours.

QUICK AS A CAT
Instantaneous reaction to an overture.

QUICK AS A MINNOW CAN SWIM A DIPPER
Rapid progress.

QUICK TURNED
A person who works and moves fast.

QUIET AS A CHURCH MOUSE
Reticent. Completely silent behavior.

R

RAIN ON YOUR PARADE
Disconcerting opinion of your planned activities.

RAISE THE ROOF
Loud noise such as a barking dog or screeching children.

RALLY ROUND THE FLAGPOLE
Patriotic gathering.

RAPPED OUT
Automobile engine operating at full throttle and approaching full speed.

RATTLING THE WINDOWS
Loud snoring.

READY AS I'LL EVER BE
Not fully prepared but proceed none the less.

READY FOR FREDDY
All set to participate in the festivities.

READY FREDDY
A person willing and able to engage in the activities at hand on a moments notice.

READY-SET-GO
Originally used as a starting chant for beginning a race. It was then shortened up and said almost as one word meaning: "Let's get moving" or "Let's get on with the show."

READY, WILLING AND ABLE
Has the ability, time, and motivation to get going on a project.

[A] REAL BARN BURNER
Exciting event.

[A] REAL KICK IN THE PANTS
Thrilling experience. Rapid acceleration.
[When our plane commander let me fly our U.S. Navy four engine aircraft it was .... I was an aerial photographer crewman on the plane at the time—1950.]

REALLY PUTTING IT AWAY
Fast, excessive food consumption.

[THE] REAL McCOY
Genuine article. Proof perfect.

RED HOT DATE
A date with a girl who you are sure you can score with.

RED SKY AT MORNING, SAILOR TAKE WARNING RED SKY AT NIGHT, SAILOR'S DELIGHT

[True more often than not, due to the fact that the red glow is the sun refracting in the ice crystals. High thick clouds made of ice crystals are part of the storm and are blown off the top of storms and precede the storms by several hours. This is why, if the red glow is in the morning to the east, you can expect stormy weather or rainy weather during the day. At night the red glow is due to the sun refracting off the ice crystals in the high clouds associated with high pressure systems. These high clouds are thin and wispy. Art Valdemar, Weatherman.]

Variation: "Red sails at morning, sailor take warning. Red sails at night, sailor's delight."

REEAR REEAR BUGS

Cicadas. Named by the sound they make.

REGULAR AS CLOCKWORK

Steady customer arriving at the same time each week. Punctual. One who has a history of making appointed rounds on time as in the case of a mailman arriving at the same time each day.

REMEMBER THE GOLDEN RULE THEM THAT HAS THE GOLD MAKES THE RULES

Money talks and carries power.

REMEMBER WELL AND BEAR IN MIND THAT AN OLD COW'S TAIL STICKS OUT BEHIND ALTHOUGH IT'S MESSY AND FULL OF BURRS SHE DOESN'T CARE BECAUSE IT'S HERS

Child's rhyme.

REPUTATION HOG

Swine whose owner gets top price bid for his stock sight unseen. This esteemed position at the marketplace is earned after a long period of sales of top-notch animals.

RICH GET RICHER AND THE POOR GET POORER

The "system" makes it harder for one of limited means to change his financial category. Our system seems destined to eliminate the middle class.
Variation: Rich get richer and the poor get children.

RIDE 'EM COWBOY

Stay on the horse. Don't give up. Being transported on a conveyance while traversing a course with a very rough surface, brings this comment from a cohort.

RIDING HIGH

Things going well. On a roll. Making money. Smooth sailing.
"He is ... now, but where will he be when the stock market crashes?"

RIDING THE BLINDS

Free rail transportation. Surreptitiously traveling the undercarriage of a train out of sight of the engineer, fireman and brakeman. [A bit noisy and dangerous I would imagine.]

RIGHT AS RAIN

True statement or belief.

RIGHT CHURCH BUT THE WRONG PEW

Correct structure but incorrect placement within. A cow who enters the milk barn then puts her head in the wrong stanchion is in the ....

RIGHT HAND DOESN'T KNOW WHAT THE LEFT HAND IS DOING

Often refers to business ventures where two opposing projects are being implemented without prior knowledge of the situation. An example would be one crew installing new doors on a building that is scheduled to be torn down by another crew.

RIGHT HERE AT YOU

One who lives or works nearby.
"Give me a whistle if you need anything, I'm ...."

RIGHT THERE IN FRONT OF GOD AND EVERYBODY

Overt unconventional behavior. Not long on modesty.
"When I did find him, he was on the town square drinking from a bottle of whiskey ...."

RIVER RAT

A person with a penchant for aquatic pursuits.

ROCKING CHAIR MONEY

Retirement pay.

ROLLED AROUND IN THERE LIKE A PEA IN A REFEREE'S WHISTLE

Used to indicate feelings after being involved in an automobile accident which rolled the vehicle with you inside.

ROLL UP THE SIDEWALKS AT DARK

A small town with no night life.

ROLL YOUR EYEBALLS

Take a look at that. Pay attention visually.
"... it's right under your nose."

ROME WASN'T BUILT IN A DAY

Ambitious projects take time.

ROMP IT

Accelerate an automobile rapidly.

ROOSTER—PULLET—HEN

Point to another's forehead, nose and chin in that order and say .... Then point to the nose again and say "what did I say that was?" When the answer, "pullet," is received you pull the nose of the other player. Play only once per person.

ROOTED RIGHT IN

Came over to our table and sat down without invitation. (Rooted like a hog in a potato patch.)

ROTTEN TO THE CORE

A person depraved to the point that reform is out of the question.

ROUGHER THAN A COB

A tough situation. Refers to the days when corncobs were used in place of toilet tissue. The Sears and Roebuck catalog was a marvelous innovation and tremendous improvement over the corncob.

ROUGH ON RATS

An encounter violent in nature.

ROUND AND ROUND SHE GOES AND WHERE SHE STOPS NOBODY KNOWS

Borrowed from the carnival pitch man's chant as he spins the wheel of fortune. Meaning changed somewhat to denote we are farming (a form of gambling) the same old way but the outcome is never certain.

RUBBING ELBOWS WITH THE ELITE

Attending a fancy party.

RUBBING SALT IN THE WOUND

To further aggravate a situation by incessantly delving back into the wrong which created the problem.

RUM BUM BASE

Answer to a tantrum or an outburst of anger by a child. What you are doing is unnecessary.

RUN IN ON A FELLOW

Said of one who constantly borrows your tools. An incessant borrower will ... every time he needs something you have.

RUN (RAN) INTO A BRICK WALL

Insurmountable obstacle. Tangling with a powerful, obstinate person as you work your way up the chain of command.

RUNNING AROUND HALF NAKED

Scantily clad. Daughter in bikini is told to put some clothes on and stop ....

RUNNING AROUND LIKE A CHICKEN WITH ITS HEAD CUT OFF

Disorganized, confused. Activity without planning. Also a person on a course of action too fast, incautious. Note: A chicken, after being beheaded, will continue to jump about.

RUNNING AWAY WITH ITSELF

Ungoverned engine turning at extremely high speed.

RUNNING HOT AND COLD

Changing directions abruptly. Deal going sweet and sour alternately. Frequent change of mind.

RUNNING IN CIRCLES

Activity with lack of accomplishment.

RUNNING IT IN THE GROUND

Unnecessary repetition to the point of irritating others.

RUNNING LIKE A SEWING MACHINE

Engine performing smoothly. Hitting on all eight. Used to describe any machine with an internal combustion engine that is operating to perfection.

RUNNING OUT OF STEAM

Tiring at the end of a long hard day.

RUNNING OUT OUR EARS

Abundance of product.
"We've got so many unsold tomatoes, they're ...."

RUN THAT BY ME ONE MORE TIME
Repeat, I don't understand. I find that hard to believe.
Reiterate, rehash.

RUSTLE UP SOME GRUB
A command to prepare a meal.

S

SACKING WILDCATS AND RAN OUT OF SACKS
Answer to a query as to one's injuries.
"How on earth did you get so skinned up?" "...."

SALLY GOODUN
Female with a very good personality and sense of humor.

SAME OLD SIXES AND SEVENS
Repetitious endeavor.

SAVE ME, SPARKS, I'M GOING DOWN WITH THE SHIP
Mock anguish and despair.
Note: "Sparks" is a nickname for the radio operator of a ship.

SAWING OFF LOGS
Soundly sleeping and snoring.

SAY PRETTY PLEASE
Precursory statement indicating your request has already been granted.
"I will do the dishes if you will ...."

SCAREDY BRITCH
Fraidy cat. Afraid of one's shadow.
Capable of being unnecessarily alarmed.
Variation: Scaredy Britches.

SCATTERED ALL OVER CREATION

As tools are found after the use of another. Parts of a plane after a serious crash.

SCATTERED LIKE RABBITS

Rapid departure by a group.
[As a volunteer firefighter, I had just arrived at a house fire. As I got out of my truck, a propane gas tank sitting next to the house exploded, throwing debris into a crowd that had gathered to watch the fire. After the explosion they .... The house was a total loss, but neighbors pitched in with money and labor and rebuilt the house for the lady since she had no insurance.]

SCATTER TO THE FOUR WINDS

Widely dispersed.

SCRAPE OFF THE BARNACLES

Shower bath.
After a long hot day in the fields it sure does feel good to ... with a hot shower.

SCRAPE THE MOSS OFF MY FANGS

Brush teeth.
It doesn't take long after getting up in the morning before the urge to ... takes over.

SCRAPING THE BOTTOM OF THE BARREL

Making do with inferior quality due to shortage of supply. Picking the last tomatoes of the season.

SCRATCH EGGS

Eggs from hens allowed to roam freely and fed hen scratch. Hen Scratch—Mixed grains fed to hens on the ground or in the litter as opposed to a complete feed ground and mixed by a mill and fed in feeders.

SCRATCH HER EYES OUT

Woman's threat to another woman who is sloe-eyeing her man.

"If she dances that way with my husband one more time I'll ...."

SCREW LOOSE IN THE UPPER STORY

Deteriorated mental ability.
Mentally unbalanced.
"The way he acts I think he has a ...."

SCUM OF THE EARTH

A lowly person.

SEAT OF THE INFECTION

Facetiously refers to the home place, main ranch, head office or any center of activity. Also any space occupied by a boss.

SECOND GO AROUND

Replanting a crop where the first did not succeed.
Twice married, once divorced.

SECRETARY'S LIP

One who practices talkative restraint.
One who does not reveal secrets they are privy to as a result of their employment has a ....

SEEMED LIKE A GOOD IDEA AT THE TIME

Hindsight observation of a mistake in judgment.

SEEN BETTER DAYS

Past glorious—future bleak.
Old, worn-out farm machinery has ....

**SEE THE LUCKY LIGHTNING BUG
WHO DOESN'T CARE A BIT
CAUSE WHEN HE SEES A TRAFFIC COP
HIS TAILLIGHT'S ALWAYS LIT**

Childhood rhyme.

SEE THE WHAT'S IN THEIR EYES

The look on someone's face as he is thinking, "What's that!"

SEE YOU AROUND

Parting words to a friend.

Variation: "See you around like a golf ball if you don't get teed off."

SEE YOU LATER

Parting message to a friend.

Answer: "It'll be later when I do see you again."

SEE YOU MADE IT ALL IN ONE PIECE

Greeting after return from a journey.

SEIZURE LATER

A crude variation of "see you later."

SELLING LIKE HOTCAKES

Merchandise moving well.

SELL IT OUT FROM UNDER YOU

Imminent purchase unexpectedly goes to another.

Your rented property sold without giving you a chance to buy it.

SENSELESS AS THEY COME

Not much regard for one's intelligence. Not too bright. Lacking aptitude.

SEPARATE THE MEN FROM THE BOYS

A group working on a very difficult task which some will not accomplish.

SHADE TREE MECHANIC

Unprepared in knowledge or equipment to do repairs but does them anyway. Refers to one who does not have a shop building and repairs equipment under the spreading branches of a tree.

SHADY CHARACTER

Person with a history of crooked dealings.

SHAKE A STICK AT

The last part of a sentence indicating abundance. "He's got more money than you can ...."

SHAKE IT EASY

Parting comment to a male friend. Debasement of the parting phrase, "take it easy".

SHAKING LIKE A LEAF

Shivering from fright or cold. "After the accident I was ...."

SHAKING IN THEIR BOOTS

Frightened. If you are superior, your adversaries are probably ....

SHAPE UP OR SHIP OUT

Perform or go elsewhere for your area of endeavor. Employed wife to unemployed husband says, "...."

SHARP AS A TACK

A person who is very intelligent, alert or perceptive.

SHARPEN YOUR PENCIL

Figure a deal with a very narrow profit margin.

SHAVE AND A HAIRCUT TWO BITS

Singsong chant meaning: So what. So what else is new.

SHEEP LEGS

Residue of child's dripping, runny nose.

SHE LOOKED AT ME LIKE I HAD JUST CRAWLED OUT FROM UNDER A ROCK

Withering stare brought on by some major social error.

SHE LOOKS LIKE A SACK FULL OF BOBCATS

Voluptuous woman in tight fitting dress.

SHE'S A FORGIVING OLD BIRD
Trustworthy airplane, easy to fly. She will allow your mistakes and let you live to tell about them.

SHE'S A GOOD LOOKING HEIFER
Attractive young woman.

SHE'S OLD ENOUGH TO SLEEP BY HERSELF
Said after checking the teeth to determine the age of an old mare.

SHINY AS A NEW DOLLAR
Brightly furbished. A new car freshly cleaned and waxed. Refers to silver dollar.

SHIPS THAT PASS IN THE NIGHT
Big feet.

[THE] SHIRT RIGHT OFF HIS BACK
A caring person who is quick to offer assistance right down to the clothing he wears if necessary.
"He would give you ...."

SHIRTTAIL FULL
Small load of grain brought in to the elevator for sale. Also used for other products like wood carried in a conveyance at less than capacity.

SHIRTTAIL OPERATION
Making ends meet operating a small business.

SHOOT LUKE—YOU GOT THE GUN
Get it over with.
Admitting that others have taken control of your destiny.
"As the judge prepares to pronounce sentence, the guilty defendant is heard to murmur ...."

SHORT END OF THE STICK
Raw deal. Didn't get fair share when the spoils were divvied up.

SHORT TIME LIVIN'—LONG TIME DEAD
Span of life on earth compared to eternity.

SHOWING OUT
Exuberant behavior to attract attention.
Usually used with reference to the actions of children.
Variation: Showing off; a show-off.

SICK AS A GOOSE
Illness that threatens to put one to bed.

SICK AS A HORSE
Bedridden with illness.

SICKER CATS THAN THAT HAVE LIVED
You'll get over it. Rectifiable mistake. Damage has been done, but it is reparable.
[Charlie was helping me build our first new home at 1117 W. Battlefield Road, Springfield, Missouri, in 1952. He had made a pattern board and cut all the studs for the bathroom from this pattern board. After we had nailed them together and we were ready to raise the wall sections into place, I noticed they were one foot shorter than the rest of the walls in the house. Charlie looked at the sections for a moment and said "...."]

SICK IN THE HEAD
One who espouses degenerate thoughts. Crazy.

SICKLING (CYCLING) RIGHT ALONG
Moving forward smoothly and expeditiously.

SIGHT ON EARTH
Amazed.
"Why, it's a ... the way he carries on."

SIGNING YOUR LIFE AWAY
Affixing a signature to an obligating document such as a mortgage which ties you up for a long time.

SI GOGLIN

Crosswise. Cater-cornered. Angled away from a direct course. Not square with the world.

[THE] SILENCE WAS DEAFENING

An ill-considered remark brings a total cessation of auditory response.

SINCE DAY ONE

Experience that goes back a long way in time.
"He has been wearing that same old Stetson ...."

SINCE HELL WAS A PUP

A long time ago.
Long separation from an old friend.
"I haven't seen him ...."

SING A SOLO—SO LOW, I CAN'T HEAR IT

Not exactly thrilled with one's performance as a singer.

SIT BACK AND ENJOY THE RIDE

After hard work and preparation is complete, the reward follows.

SIT ON YOUR FIST AND LEAN BACK ON YOUR THUMB

Answer to a request for seating space.

SITTING AROUND WATCHING THE RAIN GAUGE FILL UP

Precipitation prevents field work.

SITTING THERE LIKE A BUMP ON A LOG

Inactivity when action is needed.

SIT UP AND TAKE NOTICE

Revelation of facts that attract the attention of another.
"That will make them ... when I tell my story."

SIX BOTTLE RIDE

Gauging the length of a trip by the number of beers usually

consumed while in transit. [The friend who used this phrase died of alcohol related illness in his forties.]

SIX ONE WAY, HALF DOZEN THE OTHER
Go either way, the result is the same.

SKAT—SHOO—BEAT IT
Go away and leave me alone.
Said as one word to a younger pestering sibling.

SKID LID
Motorcycle rider's helmet.

SKINNY AS A RAIL
Very thin, emaciated, willowy.

SKIRTS ARE CLEAN
Innocent of any wrong doing.

[THE] SKY'S THE LIMIT
There are no bounds if you are determined.
In a table stakes poker game ....

SLACKING OFF
Rain letting up.
Chickens' production level dropping.
"Since those hens went into a molt they are really ... in egg production."

SLACK OFF
Stop pestering. Back off. Let up on him.
"Aw, he's just a kid, ... on him."

SLEEPING LIKE A LOG (ROCK)
Soundly snoozing.

SLEEPY DIRT
Eye contamination after slumber.

SLEPT OUT

Adequate slumber.
A condition where further sleep is impossible at this time.

SLICE 'EM THIN, SURE TO WIN

Refers to the cutting of a deck of cards preparatory to dealing.

SLICK AS AN EEL

Very slippery surface such as an ice covered highway or street. Surface devoid of traction.
Variation: Slick as a gut.

SLIPPED UP ON MY BLIND SIDE

Abrupt appearance of someone unexpectedly.
Bumping into someone as you turn around.
"I about jumped out of my skin when he ...."

SLIP YOUR COOKIES

To vomit.

SLOBBERING AT THE MOUTH

To ogle in admiration.

SLOW AS MOLASSES IN JANUARY

Less than rapid progress.
Movement of an employee about to be fired.

SLOW AS THE SEVEN YEAR ITCH

Work progressing at a snail's pace.

SLOW BOAT TO CHINA

Any slow moving vehicle.

SLOW BURN

Getting madder by the minute.
"At the party as he frolicked with the pretty young thing, I could see his wife doing a ...."

SLOW BUT SURE
Steady progress. Speedy movement sometimes results in less than desired results.

SLOW ON THE UPTAKE
Dull witted. Retarded assimilation capability.

SLY LIKE A FOX
Description of one who is very crafty or deceptive.

SMALL WORLD, ISN'T IT?
Common acquaintances from far away places.

SMART AS A WHIP
Precocious child.

SMELLS LIKE A BYGOD
The body odor of an unsanitary person.

SMOKE FOLLOWS BEAUTY
This statement made by the person in a group sitting around a campfire who is downwind.

SMOKES LIKE A CHIMNEY
Heavy indulgence in cigarettes may cause this statement to be said about you.

SMOOTH MOVE CLYDE
A cool cat. A lover with gentle tactics.

SNAKES IN THE BOOTS
Imaginary fear. As in the case of a person with the delirium tremors.

SNEAKY FOOD
Cookies or candy or other morsels that are good to eat, but not good for you.

SNOT LOCKER
Nose. "I'll punch you in the ...."

SNOWING DOWN SOUTH
Lady's slip is showing below the skirt hem line.

SNUG AS A BUG IN A RUG
Comfortably covered.

SOBER AS A JUDGE
Abstainer. A non-partaker of intoxicants. Somber.

SO HUNGRY I COULD EAT A HORSE
Famished.

SOLID AS A ROCK
Tightly fastened, secure. Denotes security such as a well set corner fence post. A person of good reputation. Pillar of the community.

SOLID AS THE ROCK OF GIBRALTER
Honest. Financially secure.

SOMEBODY WALKED OVER MY GRAVE (SITE)
Said after a shudder or shiver.

SOME DAYS IT DON'T HARDLY PAY TO GET UP
Bad day all around.

SOME EAT TO LIVE
OTHERS LIVE TO EAT
Consumption of food by some considered an entertaining, pleasurable pastime. By others only a necessity to sustain life.

SOME OF THEM THE SIZE OF MARBLES AND THE REST OF THEM LITTLE OLD BITTY THINGS
Jokingly talking about the size of fruit or vegetables being harvested.

SOMETIMES IT'S A LONG TIME A-COMIN'
Persistence pays off with perseverance in many areas such as fame, success, prosperity and happiness.

SOMETIMES WE LET OUR SKIMMER LEAK
Poor results due to sloppy management.
Refers to the skimming of cream from milk.

SON OF A BISCUIT-EATER
Mock profanity.

SOON'S IT FAIRS UP A MITE
Awaiting a break in the weather so work can resume.
"... we'll go back to pickin' strawberries."

SORRY ABOUT THAT
Said with a smile after an intended slight. Sometimes used after a physical encounter such as stepping on a friend's toe accidentally.

SORRY STATE OF AFFAIRS
Conditions intolerable.

SOUND AS A DOLLAR
A horse in very good condition.

SOUNDS LIKE A BUNCH OF MAGPIES
Group of shrieking chattering children.

SOUNDS LIKE A THRESHING MACHINE
Automobile engine making strange loud noises as it runs.

SOUP STRAINER
Mustache.

SOUR NOTE
Relationship or business deal that went bad. Conclusion of a deal with bad feelings. Activity that ends with less than desirable results.
"The wedding ended on a ... when the bride didn't show up."

SO WET WE HAD TO PLANT WITH A SHOTGUN
Soil too wet to work with tillage equipment.

SO WE WON'T HAVE TO HUNT ALL OVER HELL'S HALF ACRE FOR IT

Reminder to put an object back in its usual resting place after use.

SO WHAT ELSE IS NEW?

Tell me something I don't already know.

SPARK AS BLUE AS A POSSUM'S TAIL

Used when checking an engine to see if fire is getting to the sparkplugs. The blue electrical charge passing between the points of a sparkplug indicates a hot firing plug. A weak charge by contrast would be of a reddish tint.

SPEAK OF THE DEVIL

Said to someone who arrives just as you and a friend are talking about him. Often preceded by, "Well ...."

SPEAKS WITH AUTHORITY

A large throaty sounding engine running well and carrying heavy load easily.

SPEECH IS SILVERN, BUT SILENCE IS GOLDEN

Do not tell all you know—especially derogatory information about someone.

SPEED DEMON

One who habitually drives an automobile fast.

SPENDING LIKE IT WAS GOING OUT OF STYLE

Liquid assets rapidly declining.

SPINNING YOUR WHEELS

Non productive endeavor.

SPIT BATH

Cursory cleansing of the body.
Specifically, bathing with a sink of water and a washrag, instead of getting into a tub or under a shower.
"I was in such a hurry I just took a ...."

SPITTING MARBLES

So cold one imagines his ambeer freezing before it hits the ground.

SPITTING NAILS

Mad, irritated, agitated, vehemently verbal.
Mad enough to bite nails.

SPLITTING THE BREEZE

Fast movement. Usually refers to a rapidly moving automobile.

SPOIL THEM WHILE THEY'RE YOUNG; IT DOESN'T COST SO MUCH

Lavish small babies with gifts while it is cheap to do so.

SPOT HIM A MILE OFF

Recognizing a shady character before he gets close enough to open his mouth.

SPRING IS JUST AROUND THE CORNER BUT IT'S A BIG CORNER

As a late winter storm swirls around the house and the seed catalogs are studied a person is apt to say ....

SPUD LOCKER

A cellar or basement where potatoes and root crops are stored for the winter. Sometimes used to describe any other space where the temperature is controlled to protect from both heat and cold.

SQUALLED LIKE A MASHED CAT

Impromptu verbal explosion. Cry of anguish as a result of a hurt, physical or mental.
[I once gave a boy a small pumpkin while his mother was buying other produce. The boy's sister ... and said, "I want one too."]

SQUARE WITH THE WORLD

A structure set straight with reference to latitude and longitude.

[THE] SQUEAKING WHEEL GETS THE GREASE

Make your wants known verbally.
Complaining gets results.
Variation: The squeaking wheel gets the grease—or gets changed.

STANDING HERE WITH THE PHONE GROWING OUTA MY EAR

Being put on hold when making a telephone call.

STAND ON A DIME AND TELL WHETHER IT IS HEADS OR TAILS

Thin shoe soles bring this comment.

STARK RAVING MAD

Used facetiously to describe lack of good judgment.
"You mean to tell me you paid one thousand dollars for that junk heap? You must be ...."

STARVE A COLD—STUFF A FEVER

Oldtimer's suggested treatment for two common ailments.
[One theory is that as food enters the digestive process, blood is drawn from other parts of the body toward the intestine, resulting in a temporary cooling effect on the outer parts.
If you have a cold and a fever at the same time, consult your physician.]
Variation: Starve a cold—feed a fever.

STATUS UNATUS

Stateside. United States of America.
Used by U.S. military personnel overseas when they yearn to return to ....

STAY IN THE BUGGY

Don't despair at the adversities of life.
Mount to the challenge. Ride it out.
Modern version: Keep on truckin' (1983).

STAY UNTIL THE LAST DOG IS DEAD

Staying until the end of the party.
The final participant of a festive occasion.

STEADY BY SPURTS (JERKS)

A job that entails periods of hard work followed by periods of inactivity.

STEAL YOU BLIND

To take property right down to your eyeglasses if you are not careful. Often refers to buying and selling.

STEP AND FETCH IT

A person who runs errands and does menial chores.
Flunky.

STEP ON THAT ONE MORE TIME, YOU DIDN'T QUITE KILL IT

Said when someone blows his nose loudly.

STEPPING HIGH, WIDE AND HANDSOME

Riding high. Ostentatious cavorting. Cutting a wide swath.

STEPPING ON TOES

To interrupt or embarrass. Rebuke.
Also used to describe efforts to discourage someone from bidding at an auction.

STICKER BUSH

Any low growing plant or shrub with thorns.
A good example of a ... is a multiflora rose.

STICK OUT LIKE A SORE THUMB

Obtrusive. Contrastingly obvious.
"With that get up on you'll ...."

STICK OF WOOD

Piece of xylem fuel 16 to 24 inches long for stove or fireplace. "It's getting chilly; you had better put a ... on the fire."

STICKS AND STONES MAY BREAK MY BONES, BUT WORDS WILL NEVER HARM ME

Say what you will about me; it will amount to about the same thing as water rolling off a duck's back. Popular in the 1930s among children.

STICK YOUR FOOT IN YOUR MOUTH

Verbal error.

STIFF AS A BOARD

Anything unbending.
Jeans frozen before they dry while hanging on an outside clothesline in subfreezing temperatures become ....

[AND] STILL GOING STRONG

Getting up in years, but production continues unabated.

STILL KICKING

I am all right, alive, okay.
Answer to the question: "How are you?" "...."

STILL WATERS RUN DEEP

A quiet person with traits of honesty, integrity, and dependability is described with this phrase.

STILL WET BEHIND THE EARS

Very immature adult.

STOLEN RIGHT OUT FROM UNDER YOUR NOSE

Watching your possessions sometimes isn't enough.
Applies to anything from missing material goods to a purloined lover.

[THE] STONES IN THE STREET HATE A THIRTEEN-YEAR-OLD BOY

Degrading words to introduce a young man to teenagehood.

One reaction to the ways of a male child in his first teenage year.

STOP, TAKE A DEEP BREATH, COUNT TO THREE AND BACK UP

Use this advice when you see an argument deteriorating into a full blown fight.

STOP THE WORLD, I WANT TO GET OFF

Let's slow the pace and relax.
Trying to cope with the hectic pace of everyday life sometimes brings frustration.

STORM A-BREWING

Inclement weather imminent. Frequently used as animals are observed running excitedly for no apparent reason. Also used figuratively.

STORY OF MY LIFE

A common unfortunate past.
A person relates a tale of woe and you say, "The ...."

STOUT AS A BULL

Impressive strength. Usually used in reference to a muscular man.

STRAIGHT AS AN ARROW

Honest. Sometimes said only as "straight arrow."

STRAIGHT AS A STRING

A highway, crop row or fence that is an exact line.
Comes from marking a row for planting by stretching a string.

STRAIGHT FROM THE HEART

Sincere, loving message or action.

STRAIGHT FROM THE HORSE'S MOUTH

Getting at the source of the information. The ungarbled truth. "This is not gossip, it is ...."

STRAIGHT SKINNY

Unadulterated news. No lie. In the military where rumors run rampant at times, the ... is not hearsay, it is the absolute truth.

[THE] STRAW THAT BROKE THE CAMEL'S BACK

The last item before failure.

STRONG BACK AND A WEAK MIND

Engaged in endeavor requiring much physical labor but little intelligence brings the remark, "I'm sure glad I have a ...."

STRONG ENOUGH TO WALK

Very black coffee.

STRONG SILENT TYPE

Quiet, trustworthy, steadfast, but not vocal in his convictions.

STUBBORN AS A MULE

Unyielding in views and actions. Will not listen to opposing opinions. Can't be budged. Set in one's ways. Balky.

STUD DUCK

A big shot and knows it. Not necessarily a leader but is in a leadership position.

STUDY YOUR PROFESSOR AS CLOSELY AS YOU STUDY YOUR BOOKS

Capitalize on instructor's penchant to drop hints as to what material is important enough to be used in the testing later. Advice upon entering college.

SUCKED UP

Rapid removal of merchandise from the shelves.
We gather, wash and grade the eggs and the customers keep them ... as fast as we place them on the shelves.

SUCKER FOR PUNISHMENT

Masochistically inclined. A person running for a non-paying City Council seat is most certainly a ....

SUCKING THE HIND TIT

Slow poke. The last one in a procession of people or animals. Refers to dining place of the runt pig of a litter.

SUITS ME TO A "T"

Well pleased with the turn of events.

SUNDAY SOIL

Land which by its physical characteristics dries out rapidly, thus making it too wet to cultivate on Saturday and too dry on Monday.

SUNDOWN FARMER

A tiller of the soil who holds a steady job in town and must perform farm work in the evening hours.

SURE AS I DROP MY HAT ON THE GROUND AND DON'T DROP DEAD

Firmly convinced that what I say is true.
"I'm telling you the truth as ...."

SURE AS SHOOTIN'

Inevitable event about to take place.

SURE DO KNOW HOW TO HURT A FELLOW

Intentional or not, your actions and words have made me feel bad.

SURE ENOUGH?

Are you telling me the truth?

SURELY BY NOW

Overdue.
"... he has passed mile marker 176 and will be home in a few minutes."

SWALLER (SWALLOW) THE BITS

Eating too fast.
Activity progressing at a pace faster than necessary.
Bit referred to here is the steel part of a bridle inserted in the mouth of a horse.

SWALLOWED A WATERMELON SEED

Pregnant woman near parturition.
"She looks like she ...."

SWALLOW YOUR PRIDE

To condescend.
"... and admit that your children who are cast from your mold have not performed to your expectations."

SWAPPING SPIT

A very wet lip contact between two people.
Necking. A French kiss.

SWAT IN THE KISSER

Slap in the face.

SWAT IN THE SNOT LOCKER

Punch in the nose.

SWEAT BATH

Body covered with perspiration after exertion in high temperatures.

SWEEP IT UNDER THE RUG

A cover-up of a scandal would be a way to ....

SWEET SMELL OF SUCCESS

Personal financial goals have been achieved.

SWELL UP LIKE A POISONED PUP

Swollen. After-effects of a bee sting about a person's face makes one ....
Young dogs in their lackadaisical approach to life often come in contact with poisonous snakes which bite them, causing a puffed up place on the body.

SWERVE 'EM

Deception. Use of fabrication in a sales pitch. To divert one's attention during a deal to your advantage. To lead off the track so as to better your position.

SYMPATHY CHIT

Imaginary permit to allow someone to cry. "Don't cry the blues to me; here's a ...."

T

TAIL END CHARLIE

Last plane on a sortie.
Used to indicate the last one of any procession.

TAILOR MADES

Cigarettes bought in a pack versus hand rolled.
This term also used in the U.S. Navy to describe uniforms that are not regulation.

TAIL WAGGING THE DOG

Attempted influence or control that won't work.
"One congressman who thinks that by his influence he can sway the whole congress is the ...."

TAKE A CANE TO

To punish by force.
"If he knew I was going out with his daughter he'd ... me."

TAKE A GANDER AT THE GAMS ON THAT BABE

Calling attention, with admiration, to a lady with good-looking legs.

TAKE A LOAD OFF YOUR FEET

Come sit a spell.

TAKE AN OLD COLD TATER AND WAIT

Supper isn't ready yet.

TAKE ANOTHER STAB AT IT
Remount the attack. Repeat effort after a failure.

TAKE A WALK
Leave me alone. I do not wish to be bothered by your presence.

TAKE HIM DOWN A PEG OR TWO
Deflate the pompous with a disparaging remark.

TAKE IT EASY
Parting comment meaning relax, enjoy yourself and don't work too hard.

TAKES ALL KINDS TO MAKE A WORLD
Others have ways or views different from yours.

TAKES THE STARCH OUT OF YOU
Energy depletion due to vigorous exercise.
A put-down by another ....

TAKES TO THAT LIKE A DUCK TAKES TO WATER
Adapting to a new situation readily. Happy with a new set of circumstances. Natural involvement due to aptitude.

TAKE THE BITTER WITH THE SWEET
Philosophical approach to the adversities of life.
Coming home from the hospital to a mess at home.

TAKE THE EDGE OFF
A snack to appease the appetite temporarily.

TAKE TWO, THEY'RE SMALL
Put on your plate what you need, we have plenty.
Said to a guest but has no relationship to the size of the portion.

TAKE YOUR OLD SWEET TIME
Way to say hurry up. Sarcastic.

TALKED MY ARM OFF

The recipient of a one-sided conversation describes the incident by saying, "He darn near ...."

TALKING A MILE A MINUTE

Excited chatter. A conversation bubbling with enthusiasm.

TALK IS CHEAP

Grandiose verbal plans cost little.
He said, "I have plans to make a million dollars."
"Well, as you know, ..."
Variation: ... but it takes money to buy good whiskey.

TALKS A PRETTY GOOD FIGHT

Bragging.

TALKS OUT OF BOTH SIDES OF HIS MOUTH

Makes contradictory promises to different people.
Covers both sides of the fence while riding same.
Verbal inconsistency. Wishy washy.
"He must be a politician; he ...."

TALL DRINK OF WATER

Above average height and slender.
Male or female with a long body.
"She's a ... and skinny as a rail."

TANKING UP

Quenching one's thirst. Drinking until full before going to the field to work.

TAUGHT ME A THING OR TWO

Lesson learned the hard way.

TEAMED A LOT

A person who makes most of his living working a pair of horses on hire to others.

TEAR OUT THE BONE

Approaching a job with vigor.

TEED OFF
Mad, unhappy, angry.

TEET AND NIDY
A transpositional spoonerism for neat and tidy.

TELEPHONE TELEGRAPH TELLAWOMAN
Three fastest methods of communication.

TELL IT LIKE IT IS
The truth and nothing but the truth. Leave out the fabrication.

TELL ME ABOUT IT
I have had the same trials and tribulations. Misery loves company. This is used after someone recites a tale of woe and you have experienced same. You are not asking them to repeat the story but acknowledging that you understand by reason of experience.

TELL THE MISTER HELLO
Parting statement to a woman visitor whose husband is a friend of yours, but is not with her at the time.

TEMPTING FATE
Living dangerously.
Mowing hay while thunderstorms loom is most certainly ....

TEN TENS
Tennis shoes or sneakers.

THAN A DOG KNOWS IT'S SUNDAY
Ignorant of the facts. Oblivious.
[A friend of mine through some financial dealings ended up owning a small bank. After divesting himself of the bank he said, "I didn't know any more about running a bank ...."]

THANKS A MILLION
A hearty response to a very special favor.

THANKS FOR THE VISIT
Goodbye and come again as soon as you can.

THANK YOU KINDLY
Earnest, sincere gratitude.

THAR SHE LIES
After a long quest a lost item is found.

THAT AIN'T ALL BAD
Circumstances having adverse effects but also beneficial to some degree. Rainfall on a field of new mown hay that also waters a thirsty cornfield nearby.

THAT AIN'T HAY
A large amount of money or a nice profit.

THAT AIN'T TO BE SNEEZED AT
A generous amount. A good offer of money for an item.

THAT AIN'T TOO SHABBY
An excellent performance brings this retort from an admiring friend who doesn't want to appear too complimentary, but nonetheless is very proud of your accomplishment.

THAT AIN'T TOO SWIFT
Poor performance. Misfortune.
Opposite of "that ain't too shabby."

THAT ANSWERED THAT QUESTION
Query is replied to before it is asked.
[I told a visiting young lady that our mother cat was going to have kittens, to which she replied, "We have a dog and do not need a kitten." .... In this case the question was only implied. (Do you want a kitten?)]

THAT BREAKS AN EGG IN ME
Sarcastic reply to a not so funny joke.

THAT COVERS A MULTITUDE OF SINS
A blanket term such as Watergate.

THAT CRACKS ME UP
A very funny experience brings uncontrolled laughter and exuberance.

THAT DID (DOES) IT
You have gone past the point of reason. I will stand for no more of that.

THAT DID MY OLD HEART GOOD
An unexpected compliment brings this muse.
Seeing one get what he deserves in the way of overdue punishment.

THAT DON'T CUT IT
Inadequate performance. Doesn't make the grade. Quality of work unacceptable.

THAT DON'T LOOK HALF BAD
Pleasant in appearance.

THAT FIGURES
Not surprised at the bad news.

THAT GOES WAY BACK
Recollection of an event far in the past.

THAT KID'LL BE THE DEATH OF ME YET
Parent's comment about obstreperous teenager.
"... if she doesn't quit staying out all night."

THAT KNIFE WOULDN'T CUT HOT BUTTER
Dull as a froe. Very dull slicing instrument.

THAT LITTLE BOOGER
Light mischief by a youngster gets one this name.
"... has been in the cookie jar again."

THAT'LL COST AN ARM AND A LEG
A very high price for goods or services.

THAT'LL CURE WHAT AILS YOU
Healing potion administered. Usually refers to an alcoholic drink.

THAT'LL CURL YOUR HAIR
Strong alcoholic drink.

THAT'LL KEEP THEM OUT OF OUR HAIR
Busy work for pesky children.

THAT'LL LEAD YOU TO AN EARLY GRAVE
Any worrying activity.

THAT'LL MAKE A NEW MAN OUT OF YOU
This is a friend's prescription ....: alcoholic drink, and then sex with a loving woman, followed by a good night of sleep.

THAT'LL MAKE YOU SLEEP ON YOUR SIDE OF THE BED TONIGHT
At the end of a physically exhausting work day one does not have the energy or inclination for sex.

THAT'LL PUT HAIR ON YOUR CHEST
Strong alcoholic drink or strong boiled coffee.

THAT'LL ROT YOUR INNARDS
Admonition to one who consumes quantities of fast food, coffee, alcohol or soft drinks.

THAT'LL SET YOU BACK ON YOUR HEELS
Stern rejection or bad news.
A strong alcoholic drink.

THAT'LL STUNT YOUR GROWTH
Coffee drinking to excess brings this comment from a friend.

THAT'LL TAKE THE WIND OUT OF YOUR SAILS
An egotist learns the truth. Deflating one's ego with unkind words.

THAT MAKES MY FEEL-BAD HURT
Empathy.

THAT ONE IS IN GEAR
Fast moving vehicle.

THAT'S A CHUNK
Large quantity of money.

THAT'S A FACT
I agree with what you say.

THAT'S A HELLAVA NOTE
Displeasure at the turn of events.

THAT'S A JONAH
One who brings failure to any group effort.

THAT'S ALL SHE WROTE—I DONE SENT YOUR SADDLE HOME
Cessation of activity. Further actions would be futile.

THAT'S A-PLENTY
Enough.
As a glass is being refilled, the desired level is reached and you say, "...."

THAT'S A PRETTY GOOD LITTLE PUMP
A long uphill bicycle trek. Also used to describe an uphill climb on foot

THAT'S FOR ME TO KNOW AND YOU TO FIND OUT
Information you ask for is none of your business.

THAT SHAKES ME UP
Seriously: Am concerned at the turn of events.
Jokingly: Your problems don't bother me at all.

THAT'S LIKE LEAVING THE FOX TO GUARD THE CHICKEN HOUSE

Beware: A wolf in sheep's clothing lingers in the wings.
Letting your best friend take your girlfriend home after he drops you off first.

THAT'S MORE LIKE IT

Production returning to normal.
Good results after a period of poor performance.
Things going better. Conditions improving.

THAT'S NOT MY BAG

Said by one who refuses to engage in activities outside his area of expertise.

THAT'S OUT

Absolutely not.
I will not do it under any circumstances.

THAT'S STARTING TO GET ON MY NERVES

Repeated irritations lead to a state of agitation.
Used in our house as teenage children's choice rock radio station is turned off.

THAT'S THE CHECKER

A new and innovative piece of equipment.

THAT'S THE CROP

All there is. Harvest is over.

THAT'S THE NAME OF THE GAME

The final object, like a basket in basketball, a run in baseball or a touchdown in football.
To a money grubber, making money is the ultimate goal and ....

THAT'S THE PITS

The worst possible situation.

THAT'S THE WAY THE BALL BOUNCES

Regrettable but unavoidable misfortune that must be lived with, so make the best of it.

THAT'S WHAT THEY MAKE KNIVES AND GUNS FOR

Equalizers.
Barroom antagonist unable to physically overcome a larger, more powerful opponent says ....

THAT WENT OVER LIKE A LEAD ZEPPELIN

A proposal or act not enthusiastically accepted.
Usually refers to a serious verbal error when speaking before a group of people.

THAT WON'T CARE

It'll feel better when it quits hurting.

THE ALTITUDE ABOVE YOU
RUNWAY BEHIND YOU
FUEL IN THE TANK AT THE AIRPORT

The three most useless things to an airplane pilot.

[AND] THE BEAT GOES ON

Business as usual
Repetitious activity.

THE DIFFICULT WE DO IMMEDIATELY,
THE IMPOSSIBLE TAKES A LITTLE LONGER

Confidence in ability. "Can do" attitude.
[Sign seen over the door of a repair shop at U.S. Naval Air Station, Pensacola, Florida, 1949.]

[AND] THE FUR FLEW

Altercation.
"I came home at two a.m. without an excuse ...."

THEM BIG BOYS GOT ME DOWN AND MADE ME DRINK IT

Excuse for a hangover.

THERE ADEE
Yonder it is.

THERE AIN'T NO JUSTICE IN THIS HERE WORLD
Justice administered by humans is full of flaws.
"Jus ain't no justice in this land;
Jus got a divorce from my ole man.
Had to laff at the judge's decision.
Gave all my kids to that ole man;
And nary a one of 'em was hisen."
C.H. Kelly

THERE AIN'T NO TWO WAYS ABOUT IT
Only one conclusion can be drawn.
Opposite of: "Well there's two ways of looking at it."
"... this is the only course of action."

THERE ARE LIARS, DAMN LIARS AND THEN THERE ARE STATISTICIANS
With proper training, fabrications can be made out of figures.

THERE ARE MORE FISH IN THE SEA
Condolatory remark to one who has lost his girlfriend.

THERE ARE ONLY TWO PEOPLE IN THE WHOLE WORLD I TRUST—YOU AND I—AND SOMETIMES I WONDER ABOUT YOU
Skeptic's choice phrase.

THERE MAY BE SNOW ON THE ROOFTOP BUT THERE'S STILL A FIRE IN THE FURNACE
Older male with ability for sexual activity. A sexy senior citizen.
This is usually said by a cocky, elderly, silver haired male.
Sometimes said about him by his wife.

THERE'S MORE WHERE THAT CAME FROM
Any action that can be repeated. Spending lavishly but adequate financial resources are still held in reserve.

THERE'S NO PERFECTION ON EARTH

Perfection awaits the heaven-bound.
Earthlings must endure an imperfect existence.

THERE'S NO SUCH THING AS A LITTLE BIT OF GARLIC

The pungency of this bulb gives it the reputation of being a powerful condiment.
"I'm going to add a little garlic to the stew." "...."

THERE'S NOT A LAZY BONE IN HIS BODY

A complimentary remark about an industrious, hard working individual.

THERE'S SOMETHING TO BE SAID FOR ...

A commonly held belief that a condition or idea is bad, but does have some good characteristics that are not readily apparent. "... being older but wiser."

THERE'S THIRTY PERCENT OF YOU I'M NOT MARRIED TO

Said to overweight husband or wife whose weight has increased significantly since marriage.

THE RUSSIANS ARE COMING, THE RUSSIANS ARE COMING

Poking fun at an overly concerned person.
A fake panic cry.

THE UNGARBLED TRUTH

The absolute truth.
The clear description of an event.
"Skip the superfluous, give me ...."

THEY BROKE THE MOLD WHEN THEY MADE HIM

Outstanding, unique individual.

•

THEY HAVE A WAY WITH ME

One who is easily manipulated by certain people.
"My beguiling daughters; ...."

THEY JUST THINK THE WORLD AND ALL OF HIM
Great respect and affection.

THEY'LL PLUG YOUR WELL
One way of seeking revenge.
[A well that is cased below the water level is fitted with a round stove length section of dry wood. The diameter is made to fit snugly inside the casing, then it is forced down to the water level where it soaks up water, swells up and lodges in the casing, rendering the well inoperative.]
"If you make serious enemies of some people in this part of the hills you had better watch out or ...."

THEY MIGHT NOT TAKE KINDLY TO THAT
Others will view your actions as objectionable.

THEY SAW YOU COMING
Fleeced. Cheated. Overcharged for goods or services.

THEY START COMING OUT OF THE WOODWORK
The appearance of others you do not wish to see.
Customers when you are about out of eggs. Bill collectors if debts become overdue.

THEY STAYED AWAY IN DROVES
Light attendance at a function.

THEY WILL BE DOWN ON YOU WITH BOTH FEET
Retribution. Warning of consequences.
"When your actions are found out ...."

THEY WILL REST EASY TONIGHT
Feeling of relief or satisfaction after a difficult success.

THINGS ARE GETTING OUT OF HAND
Control of the situation is lost.

THINGS ARE LOOKING UP
Trial and tribulation behind us now and all is well.
Happy days are here again.

Almost out of the woods.
Outlook is for conditions to improve.

THINGS HAVE COME TO A SCREECHING HALT
Sudden cessation of activities.

THINK FAST
This is said to someone as you toss them something such as an egg.

THINK I'LL GO JUMP OFF OLD BONEY
Things are going so bad that one jokingly considers suicide. [Old Boney is a massive sandstone rock outcropping with a high precipice overlooking Jordan Creek located in Dade County, Missouri, near the town of Everton.]

THINK IT WILL RAIN? (FIRST PERSON)
ALWAYS HAS (SECOND PERSON)
A sardonic approach to an age old question.

THIRD TIME'S THE CHARM
Persistence until success.
There is this notion that good and bad things come in threes.

THIRTY DAYS HATH SEPTEMBER
APRIL JUNE AND NOVEMBER
ALL THE REST HAVE THIRTY ONE
SAVE FEBRUARY WITH TWENTY EIGHT
'CEPT LEAP YEAR, IT'S TWENTY NINE
One way to remember how many days there are in each month of the year.

THIS AIN'T MY DAY
Evening appraisal of a day spent in mass frustration.

THIS AIN'T YOUR TERRITORY
Someone in the wrong place.

THIS HAD BETTER BE GOOD
Awaiting an answer as to why.

Such as a youngster coming in three hours later than specified. Boss's remark to employee coming to work late.

THIS IS WHERE I SHINE
Something I do exceptionally well.

THIS LOOKS LIKE GRAND CENTRAL STATION
Room completely full of friends and relatives brings this remark from a late arrival.

THIS NECK OF THE WOODS
A certain area. Our community.

**THIS OLD WORLD WE'RE LIVING IN IS MIGHTY HARD TO BEAT,
YOU GET A THORN WITH EVERY ROSE BUT AIN'T THEM ROSES SWEET**
Pleasures are frequently interrupted with some of the miseries of life.

THIS WILL HURT ME MORE THAN IT DOES YOU
Spanking a loved child.

THIS WON'T TAKE LONG, DID IT
A job complete before you have time to tell about it.
This is the way we wish the dentist would perform his tasks.

THORN IN MY SIDE
Irritating factor or circumstance (usually a person) that won't go away.

THRASH YOU TO WITHIN AN INCH OF YOUR LIFE
Threat of dire punishment if you persist in your actions.

THREE TIMES RUNNING
Successive repetition.

THRILL, THRILL
Someone shows up you don't particularly want to see.
"... here comes the bill collector."

THROTTLE JOCKEY
Airplane pilot.

THROW CAUTION TO THE WINDS
Proceed dangerously with abandon.

THROWING GOOD MONEY AFTER BAD
Reinvesting in a losing venture.

THROWING STICKS ON THE FIRE
Fanning the flames of controversy.

THROWN TO THE WOLVES
One who you had supported is cut loose.

THROW THE BABY OUT WITH THE BATH WATER
Losing the values while correcting the faults.

THROW THE BOOK AT HIM
It is recommended that the culprit receives the maximum sentence for an offense.

TICKLED TO NO END
Happy. Very pleased.
"I'm just ... to hear from you."
Variation: Tickled no end.

TIE A STRING ON YOUR FINGER
Reminder of something to do in the future you are apt to forget.
[It doesn't work in my case because I tend to forget why I tied the string on my finger.]

TIED IN
Associated with, but not to your advantage.
You have become partially under the control of others.

TIED OUT
A man's secret girlfriend.
A woman who is always available to a certain man.
A woman on a string.

"You have been out every night this week; have you got something ...?"

TIE HER HANDS BEHIND HER BACK AND SHE COULDN'T TALK

Comment about the habit some people have of making gesticulative movements as they speak.

TIE PANTS

Men's jeans or trousers requiring a belt for support as opposed to bib overalls which are supported by straps over the shoulders.

TIGHT AS A BASS DRUM

Rusty nut not coming loose when wrench and pressure is applied.

TIGHT AS A FIDDLE STRING

Tension such as on a fence wire.

TIGHT AS BARK ON A TREE

Conservative with money.

TIGHT COLLAR

An expert visitor to the farm such as a county agent wearing a necktie.

TILL BETTER PAY

A kind word instead of monetary reward for a job well done. Appreciate your help and would pay you if I could.
"... I thank you for your help."

TILL THE COWS COME HOME

A long wait.

TILL THE WORLD LOOKS (LOOKED) LEVEL

Engaged in disorienting activity.
"We drank beer ...."

TIME BUILDER

A small economical airplane used to accumulate flying hours for the next step in a pilot's licensing process.

TIME IS MONEY

If you don't believe it, visit with your lawyer.

TIME'S A-WASTIN'

Daylight is slipping by.
Cooling your heels while there is work to be done.

TIRED AS A PUP

Totally exhausted.

TIRED LITTLE RAGAMUFFINS

Sleepy children.

'TIS NEITHER HERE NOR THERE

Doesn't make any difference to me.
I care not for your opinion of my actions.

TOAD STRANGLER

Rainfall so fast ground becomes covered with water.

TO ASSUME MAKES AN ASS OUT OF YOU AND ME

Be careful in your assumptions as they may make you look like a fool.

TOASTING YOUR BUNS

Backed up to the fire.

TOE JAM

Accumulation of sloughed-off skin between the appendages of the feet and under the toenails.

TO FORTIFY YOUR SOUL

Offer of a drink.

TO KEEP FROM GETTING PREGNANT, SLEEP WITH YOUR FEET IN A FRUIT JAR

Pregnant woman comes back later and says: "You didn't say both feet in one jar."

TOLD HIM WHERE TO HEAD IN

Informing someone of your opposing position. To tell off.

TOLD IT FAR AND WIDE

Your misdeeds verbalized extensively by another.
"When I got caught that old biddie ...."

TOMATO KING

Person who grows tomatoes on a large scale. In our part of the hills one acre of tomatoes would qualify a grower for this title.

TOMORROW IS ANOTHER DAY

An excuse to leave work unfinished.
Today's job incomplete.

TOMORROW NEVER COMES

At the stroke of midnight a new day makes the morrow forever elusive.

TO MY NOTION

In my opinion.
Ideas I hold dear regardless of divergent views held by others. A way of saying: "to my way of thinking."

TONGUES A-WAGGIN'

The way gossip is disseminated.
"They set their ... when she came home at daylight."

TONIGHT'S THE NIGHT

Time for sex.

TOO BIG FOR YOUR BRITCHES

One who thinks he is more important than he really is.
Usually said of a growing child.

TOO CLOSE FOR COMFORT

A near rendezvous with calamity. A narrow squeak.
Tender plants have been set out, and the temperature dips to near freezing mark.
As in a near miss between two aircraft.
As in combat: "that bullet or bomb was ...."
They are building a new highway near our home and it is ...."

TOO FAR GONE

Candidate for replacement. Beyond repair, can't be fixed.
Imminent death.

TOO GOOD TO BE TRUE

Unexpected bonanza of doubtful tenure.

TOOK A LIKIN' TO

An acquaintance becomes a friend.

TOOK A STAB AT IT

Halfhearted approach to a project.
Unenthusiastic attempt.

TOOK A TURN FOR THE WORSE

Getting sicker.
Gravely ill and death imminent.

TOOK OFF LIKE A SCALDED CAT

Rapid departure.

TOOK SICK

To come down rapidly with a malady.
"Just all of a sudden he ... and died."

TOOK SOME DOING

Difficult project completed after much effort.

TOOK THE WIND OUT OF MY SAILS

Vigorous endeavor that ends in failure.
Discovering facts that make an effort pointless.

TOOK THE WORDS RIGHT OUT OF MY MOUTH
One's verbalization of another's thought.

TOO MANY CHIEFS AND NOT ENOUGH INDIANS
More managers than workers.

TOO MANY COOKS SPOIL THE BROTH
Some projects proceed better with individual effort.
"Get out of my kitchen, ..."

TOO POOPED TO POP
Tired to the point that sexual advances by a partner are spurned. Totally exhausted.

TOO RICH FOR MY BLOOD
Too expensive.
A high stakes poker game.
Expensive endeavor, pastime, or enterprise.
Wealthy man's game.

TOOTHLESS TIGER
A being of great strength but not motivated or equipped for action.
"Has the United Nations become a ...?"

TOP OFF THE TANKS
Refill a container before it is empty.
Generally used with reference to the filling of the fuel tanks of an aircraft at an intermediate stop before they are anywhere near empty.
Last drink at a bar before closing time.

TORE UP HOB
As in the aftermath of a tornado or a brawl.

TOUGH AS A BOOT
A person resilient under stress.

TOUGH AS BUCKSKIN
Chewy meat.

TOUGH CUSTOMER
A pugnacious renegade.

TOUGH IT OUT
Wear out an illness without medication.

TOUGH NUT TO CRACK
A serious problem with no easy solution.

TOUGH SLEDDING
Hard times. Rough row to hoe.

TOURIST TRAP
Business in a recreational area catering to travelers. A place designed to separate a traveler from his money. Natives do not trade there because of the high prices and frivolous nature of the merchandise.

TRACTORS WITH LUGS PROHIBITED
State highway sign appearing on the paved roads of Missouri in the days when some farm tractors had steel pointed lugs instead of rubber tires on the rear wheels. Although offering good traction in the fields, they played havoc with pavement.

TRAIL DUST IS GETTING HEAVY IN MY THROAT
Cocktail hour approaching.

TRAIN OF THOUGHT
Uninterrupted cerebral function.

TRAVELING OR GOING SOMEWHERE?
You look as though you are departing on a journey. Someone carrying a suitcase is asked: "...?"

[THE] TRUTH HURTS
Hearing an accurate evaluation of your efforts is sometimes painful.

TUBE STEAK
A wiener of frankfurter.

TUCK TAIL AND RUN
Defeat by acquiescence. Retreat in disgrace.
Cowardice under fire.

TURKEY PEEP OVER THE LOG
Said while pulling the hair of another at the nape of the neck.

TURNED UP HIS TOES
Died.

TURN ON A DIME AND GIVE YOU NINE CENTS CHANGE
Short turning radius.

TUTHER END
To the other extremity of a field.
"As soon as we get ... we'll stop for a drink of water."
Slang for "to the other end."

'TWAS NOT I
Did not do it.

TWENTY FOUR HOURS BETWEEN THE BOTTLE AND THE THROTTLE
Navy pilots' credo.
Allowing time for the body to rid itself of alcohol so the acuity of the senses is not impaired, making flying safer.

TWO-BIT CROOK
Penny ante criminal.

TWO BRICKS SHY OF A FULL LOAD
Jokingly referring to a mental deficiency that is nonexistent.

TWO-FISTED DRINKER
Heavy consumer of alcohol. Alcoholic in training.

TWO FRECKLES PAST A HAIR
Answer when someone asks you the time of day and you

look at your wrist which has no watch attached.
Variation: Two hairs past a freckle.

TWO HEADS ARE BETTER THAN ONE
Consultation with another on a problem will frequently bring better results.

TWO SHAKES OF A COW'S TAIL
A short span of time.
"It didn't take him ... to get that old car running again."
Variation: Two shakes of a lamb's tail; ... mare's tail.

TWO TON TESSIE
Usually refers to a very obese woman.
Can refer to almost anything of enormous size or weight.

'TWOULD BE A FRIGHT
The facts would scare you.
"If you knew what was going on ...."

TWO WHOOPS AND A HOLLER
A short distance.
"How far is it?" "Oh, just ... down the road."

TWO WHOOPS IN HELL
Little worth.
"I wouldn't give ... for him."

TWO WRONGS DON'T MAKE A RIGHT
Getting even with someone seldom leaves one with a genuine sense of satisfaction.

U

UGA BOO UGA BOO BOO UGA UGA BOO BOO
Said while passing someone from behind on foot.
Same as honking horn while passing another automobile.

Use this only with friends, as others will think you are weird.

UGLY AS A BRUSH APE

Physical characteristics not conducive to attractiveness or beauty.

UNDER THE WEATHER

Sick but not to the point of being bedridden.
Slightly ill. Not up to par.

UNGLUED FROM HIS SOCKS UP

To vomit.

[THE] UNVARNISHED TRUTH

The whole ungarbled truth.
The bare facts without window dressing.

UP A CREEK WITHOUT A PADDLE

Dismal circumstances with little chance of improvement.

UP FRONT MONEY

Cash in hand before project will start.

UP HERE WE PRICE LAND BY THE SHOVEL FULL

Used in places where real estate is priced by the square foot rather than by the acre.
City cousin says this to country cousin.

UP HILL AND DOWN DALE

Looked everywhere. Rambling over the countryside.
Wandering traveler.

UP IN YEARS

Elderly.

UPS AND DOWNS

Elation and woe in varying degrees are just a part of life. In our forty years of married life we've had our ....

UPSET THE APPLE CART
A change in plans not to your liking.
Disruption of routine affairs.
"When the groom didn't show up for the wedding that ...."

UP THE RIVER
Sent to the penitentiary.

UP THE YING YANG
Abundance of monetary resources.
"He's got money ...."

UPTIGHT AND TENSE
Nervous.

V

VARIETY IS THE SPICE OF LIFE
The credo of a person with many lovers.
One of human's basic needs is the desire for new experiences. Varied activities provide an opportunity to satisfy this craving.
As when a customer wants five dozen large eggs and all we have is two medium and three extra large, we say ....

[A] VERITABLE FOUNTAIN OF INFORMATION
Intelligent, verbal person.

W

WACKY TOBACCY
Marijuana.

WAD OF BILLS ON HIM THAT WOULD CHOKE A HORSE

Person carrying a large amount of currency.

WAGON TIRES

Iron rims that go around the outside of wooden wagon wheels. [As these wagons went out of use the iron rims were sometimes removed, cut and straightened, and used as runners for sleds and repair material for farm implements. Also used as hoops for children to roll—fancier and bigger than barrel hoops.]

WAITING FOR MY SHIP TO COME IN

One who thinks someday a large sum of money will be placed in his lap.
The breaks will come my way with time.
Some tire of the wait and by hard working endeavor speed up the process.
Variation: With my luck, when my ship comes in, I'll be at the bus station.

WAITING FOR THE AX TO FALL

A person about to be fired.
Unpleasant, inevitable event forthcoming.
Period of time between guilty verdict and sentencing.
To be more specific, a chicken's neck laying on the chopping block.

WAITING IN THE WINGS

Biding one's time. Adversary patiently seeking proper time to strike.

WAKE UP AND SMELL THE COFFEE

Be observant as to what is going on around you, especially the nice things.

WAKE UP IN A NEW WORLD EVERY DAY

Lack of coordinated effort leads to a confused state of mind and perplexing issues to face each morning.
Also consolation for failure.

WALK A HOLE IN THE GROUND
A five-gaited horse performing well.

WALK AROUND IN THE HOUSE WITH ONE SHOE ON
Bad luck will follow if you ....

WALKING ENCYCLOPEDIA
One who has an abundance of information on a variety of subjects.

WALKING THE DOG
Showing off with a new set of clothes.
Puttin' on airs.

WALL TO WALL
Absolute coverage. As in a room full of children.
Sometimes used to indicate a whole farm or field planted to one crop.

WANNA BET?
I beg to differ with your position and will place a wager to prove it.
"My pa can whip your pa." "...?"

WANT A CHAW?
The offering of a plug of chewing tobacco that is limited to one serving.

WARDROBE UPDATE
Farmer in a clean pair of overalls.

WARM AS TOAST
Comfortable environmental temperature.
Sometimes refers to the effect of heavy clothing in cold weather.

WASH YOUR MOUTH OUT WITH SOAP
Child's penalty for saying a naughty word.
"If I hear you say another four-letter work, I'll ...."

WASTING AWAY

Losing weight as in the case of a debilitating illness.

WASTING YOUR AMMUNITION

The project is doomed for failure so direct your efforts elsewhere.

WATCH EVERY MOVE HE MAKES

Past experience dictates caution in future dealings with this person. Admonition to observe an untrustworthy person.

WATCH HER EYES LIGHT UP

Reaction to a pleasant situation.
"When I present this gift, ..."

WATCHING THE WORLD GO BY

In repose but vigilant to the affairs of the day. Loafing.

WATCH IT, CLYDE

Warning to a male getting too fresh.
Sometimes used as a correctional expression for smart-alecky teens.

WATCH IT, THAT MIGHT BE CATCHING

Said to a young unmarried female while she holds another's baby.

WATCH IT, YOUR HOUND(S) WILL GET OUT

Said to a male with front fly of pants partially unbuttoned or unzipped.
Also used to denote lady's plunging neckline.

WATCH YOUR PENNIES AND THE DOLLARS WILL TAKE CARE OF THEMSELVES

Small frivolous expenditures add up to large sums in time. Prudent advice to a spendthrift.

WATER GAP

A fencing device designed to partition a piece of ground traversed by a river or branch. Usually swung between two trees and free to move at the bottom to allow for high water and yet contain livestock.

WATER UNDER THE BRIDGE

Too late to do anything about it.
What's done is done.

WATER, WATER EVERYWHERE AND NOT A DROP TO DRINK

When at sea something to say to break the boredom.
[During long stretches at sea with the U.S. Navy, we used this phrase as a way of saying I wish I were sitting beside a cool Ozarks spring with a pretty young lady.]

WAY, SHAPE OR FORM (FASHION)

A set of words used to describe a definite opinion.
"In no ... can I go along with your idea."

[THE] WAY TO A MAN'S HEART IS THROUGH HIS STOMACH

In courtship good cooks have the edge.
A marriage-minded woman who excels in the kitchen holds the cards. Culinary expertise leads to easier matchmaking. This statement held more truth before the fast food craze erupted.
When she invited him to her apartment for wine and dinner, his roommate says: "...."

WEAK IN THE POOTS

Lack of strength due to previous overexertion.

WEARS ON YOU

Getting accustomed to one's ways by association.
Relationship gradually deteriorating.

WEATHER GUESSER

Meteorologist.

WE CAN HANG YOU ON A NAIL

Answer to limited sleeping space for overnight visitor.
"Do you have room for me to spend the night?" "...."

WE DIDN'T TAKE HIM TO RAISE

Unwelcome guest overstaying his welcome.
One who continually asks for favors, help or assistance with his problems and offers nothing in return.

WE DON'T CLAIM HIM

Black sheep of the family.

WE DON'T STAND ON CEREMONY AROUND HERE

Take off your coat, hat, and tie and relax.
A head of household who insists on an atmosphere of absolute informality for all visitors says, ...
Variation: We don't stand on ceremony around here, we tromp on it.

WE GONE

Citizens band radio lingo for signing off.

WELCOME TO THE CLUB

We share the same misfortunes so let us cry on each other's shoulder.
Hardships borne with comfort in the knowledge that others are in the same boat.

WE LIVED SO FAR BACK IN THE WOODS WE HAD TO SHIP IN OUR OWN TOMCAT

Remote place of habitation. Male felines range far in the pursuit of procreation, but there is a limit.

WELL? (first person)
THAT'S A DEEP SUBJECT (second person)

The first person is using the word as a question and the second either doesn't want to answer, doesn't have the answer or is being just plain smartalecky.

WELL, BLESS MY SOUL

Good fortune has befallen me.

WELL, COME ON IN

Said as someone drives up and parks extremely close to the doorway of the house.

WE'LL GET ANOTHER CRACK AT IT
Return bout. Opportunity not completely lost.

WELL, GOOD!
I appreciate the pleasant news.
After receipt of desirable information or happy results, one says, "...."

WELL, GOOD MORNING!
Walking in on someone unexpectedly while they are urinating.

WELL, I DECLARE
Amazement.

WELL, LA-TE-DA!
Who do you think you are, putting on a front to make people think you are better than we are? A person becomes a bit too sophisticated and a friend of the old days says, "...."

WELL, LOOKEE HERE!
Actually means "what have we here" with a touch of envy and sarcasm thrown in.
Someone arriving in new duds gets the greeting, "...."

WELL, I'LL BE A SON OF A SEA COOK!
Beats me. I'll be darned.

WELL, WHAT DO YOU KNOW?
Surprise at the turn of events. Usually refers to a favorable outcome.
"... That old long shot nag I bet on came in first."

WELL, WHY NOT?
Let's do it.

WE MOVED SO MANY TIMES THAT EVERY TIME A TRUCK WOULD PULL INTO THE DRIVEWAY OUR CHICKENS WOULD LAY DOWN AND CROSS THEIR LEGS
Chickens are sometimes transported in small numbers by

tying their legs together to keep them from running away. A facetious Ozarkian example of Pavlov's conditioned response theory.

WENT FROM BAD TO WORSE
Steady deterioration of conditions.

WENT TO HIS HEAD
Newly acquired power gives one a pompous attitude. Got "the big-head."

WE'RE ALL SET (TO GO)
Prepared to advance.

WE'RE IN BUSINESS
A project has gotten under way.

WE'RE KINDA SNEAKY
Adding or doing something that is not apparent. Example: We sell our eggs so fresh that we use your refrigerator to cool them.

WE'RE OFF—LIKE A HERD OF TURTLES
A slow, disorganized departure.

WE'RE OVER THE HUMP
A very difficult job past the halfway point.

WERE YOU BORN IN A BARN?
Leaving outside door to a house ajar in cold weather. "Close the door, ...?"

WERE YOUR EARS BURNING?
We were just talking about you.

WE SHALL SEE WHAT WE SHALL SEE
Pending outcome.

WET AS SOP
Dripping with sweat or rain.

WET NOODLE

A person with few social skills. One characteristic is a very limp handshake. Definitely not the life of the party.

WE'VE BROKEN THE BACK OF OLD MAN WINTER

Spring is here.

WE'VE DONE ALL THE DAMAGE WE CAN DO HERE FOR TODAY

Quitting time.

WE'VE GOT IT ON THE RUN

Malady curing. Malaise almost cured, and one is on the mend.

WE WAITED FOR YOU LIKE ONE PIG WAITS FOR ANOTHER

Going ahead and eating before someone expected arrives for a meal.

WHAT A FARMER DOESN'T KNOW HE DOESN'T EAT

A German saying meaning a farmer tends to shy away from exotic or strange foods that vary from the basic food groups.

WHAT AILS YOU?

Asked of one who is acting strange.
"Are you in your right mind; ...?"

WHAT ARE WE GOING TO DO WITH YOU?

Said to a person who repeatedly makes mistakes.
Usually a family member or a close friend.
This phrase is sometimes preceded by repeating the person's first name many times (at least three).
"John, John, John, John, ...?"

WHAT ARE YOU SO ALL FIRED UP ABOUT?

Give me one good reason for your agitation.

WHAT ARE YOU SQUAWKING ABOUT?

Why are you jawboning?
You have no reason to complain.

WHAT ARE YOU WAITING FOR—CHRISTMAS?

Get cracking.
Get a move on.
Get off your duff and on the stick.

WHAT BROUGHT THAT ON?

Inquiry as to activity or actions with no apparent reason.

WHATEVER YOUR LITTLE OL' HEART DESIRES

Your wish is but my command.

WHAT FER? (first person)
CAT FUR TO MAKE KITTEN BRITCHES (second person)

Answer when you don't admit the need for an answer.
Calling attention to one's mispronunciation of "for."

WHAT HAVE WE HERE?

Congratulatory response to mother showing off her new born baby.

WHAT IS THAT SUPPOSED TO MEAN?

Answer to a thinly veiled threat.

WHAT'LL YOU TAKE FOR IT AND NOT BACK OUT

Trying to elicit a firm bottom dollar price.
"That's a good looking horse you have there; ...?"

If you still can't get a response you say: "Would you take $100 for that horse?" Here you have protected yourself in that no actual offer to purchase has been made—only a query as to the acceptance of an offer if it is made.

Never say, "I'll give you $100," before you have received an asking price from the seller.

In horse trading these procedures must be followed carefully, for your word is your bond.

WHAT ON EARTH?
Incredulity.

WHAT'S A POOR MAN TO DO?
Woe to the unwealthy.
The avenues out of poverty are limited and frustrating.

WHAT'S COOKING?
A query as to activities in progress at the time.
A joking response is: "Bacon; wanna strip?"

WHAT'S GOOD FOR THE GOOSE IS GOOD FOR THE GANDER
Equal treatment for all concerned.

WHAT'S THE GOOD WORD?
A greeting to a friend—used in place of "hello."

WHAT'S THE HOLD UP?
Why the delay?

WHAT'S THE PROBLEM?
A supervisor returning to find a lack of progress.

WHAT'S THIS WORLD A-COMIN TO?
Observation of an old-timer with reference to the supposed depravity of today's youth.

WHAT'S YOUR HANDLE?
Citizens band radio operator's jargon asking for your over-the-air nickname.

WHAT'S YOUR PLEASURE?
Inquiry as to preference of drink.
"I'm buying, ...?"

WHAT THE HAY!
To heck with it. It matters not.
"... Go for it."

WHEN A QUARTER LOOKED AS BIG AS A CARTWHEEL

In retrospect, a one-fourth dollar coin carried quite a bit of buying power for one of limited means.
In times past, cartwheel was a nickname for a silver dollar.

WHEN HE GETS HIS HEAD ON STRAIGHT

Behavioral change will occur as the clouding of the mental process is lifted.

WHEN I GROW UP I'M GONNA NAME MY SON, CHARLIE, AND MAKE HIM HOE SWEET POTATOES ALL DAY

His way of facetiously getting even with his father, Charles, for forced child labor in the sweet potato patch.

WHEN IN ROME, DO AS THE ROMANS DO

Admonition by parent as a son or a daughter departs the farm for the big city. Fit your behavioral patterns to your new environment. Keep your eyes and ears open and your mouth shut.

WHEN SHIPS WERE MADE OF WOOD AND MEN OF STEEL

The reminiscence of an old salt.
Reference here is that nowadays men are wood and ships steel.

WHEN THE CAT IS AWAY, THE MICE WILL PLAY

Goofing off when the boss isn't around.

WHEN THE CHIPS ARE DOWN

The moment of truth. Down to the nitty-gritty.
Refers to the placing of bets in a card game where chips are used in place of money.
A true friend will not abandon your cause ....

WHEN THE DUST SETTLES

Evaluation after feverish activity.
A cooling off period after a confrontation.
"A decision will be made ...."

WHEN THE GOING GETS TOUGH, THE TOUGH GET GOING

Stamina under stress.

WHEN THE SUN PASSES THE YARD ARM

Old sailor without a watch keeping track of when to start the cocktail hour.
Yard Arm: One end of a tapered spar supporting the head of a square sail on a ship. In this case it is the end pointing toward the west.

WHEN WE GET LINED OUT

After preparations are complete, work will begin.
Usually used as a phrase of procrastination.

WHEN YOU ARE UP, THEY WILL CALL YOU CROOKED—WHEN YOU ARE DOWN, THEY WILL KICK YOU

The voice of experience telling us a very basic fact of life—in the dog-eat-dog world some find themselves in.

WHEN YOU GOT TO GO, YOU GOT TO GO

Heeding Mother Nature's call. Need to expel waste.

WHEN YOU MOVE INTO A NEW NEIGHBORHOOD, MARK OFF THE FIRST VISITOR

This is not a hard and fast rule, but usually the nosy, meddling neighbor will be the first to visit.

WHEN YOUR NOSE ITCHES

Someone is talking about you.

WHERE AM I?

Confused and disoriented after hectic activity.

WHERE DID YOU COME FROM? (first person)
MY MOMMY (second person)

Facetious answer, "my mommy," is a replacement for the usual reply of one's most recent geographic location.

WHERE DID YOU GET THAT TRASH BAG!

Indicating a woman carrying excess weight.
Said to a woman in the last trimester of pregnancy.

WHERE I COME FROM

Educating associates in new surroundings as to the behavioral code abided by in your own region.
"... gentlemen do not curse in the presence of ladies."

WHERE'S IT AT? (first person)
BEHIND THE AT (second person)

Correction in grammar (facetious answer).

WHERE THERE'S A WILL, THERE'S A WAY

Determined to see a project carried through to completion.

WHERE THERE'S SMOKE, THERE'S FIRE

I smell a rat. Something fishy going on.
Good probability of illicit activity.

WHERE WAS I?

To pick up a train of thought. Recommence a task after an interruption.

WHERE YOU BEEN KEEPING YOURSELF?

Greeting to a friend you haven't seen in a long time.

WHERE YOU GOING? (first person)
GOING TO PIECES (second person)

The reply indicates it is none of your business where I go.

WHERE YOU PREACHING TODAY?

Said to someone dressed up in a suit and tie who doesn't ordinarily do so.

WHETHER THE WEATHER BE COLD
OR WHETHER THE WEATHER BE HOT
WE'LL WEATHER THE WEATHER
WHATEVER THE WEATHER
WHETHER WE LIKE IT OR NOT

An exercise in the correct spelling of two similar sounding words.

WHICH CAME FIRST, THE CHICKEN OR THE EGG?

Unanswerable question.

WHISTLE BRITCHES

A young child.

WHITE SIDEWALLS

A very close haircut where the head is sheared clean of hair on the sides, leaving exposed the untanned skin underneath. Refers literally to white stripes on the sides of automobile tires.

WHOA, NELLIE

Wait a minute, let's take a look at that again.
Slow down, you are driving too fast.

WHO DOES HE THINK HE IS—ONE OF THE BEAUTIFUL PEOPLE?

Said about one who is arrogant and conceited without just cause.

WHO?—HELL—YOUR FOOT DON'T FIT NO LIMB

Answer to someone prying into the affairs of another by asking an identity unnecessarily.
"Who was that on the phone?" "...."
"Who" refers to the sound made by a hoot owl which clutches tree branches with its feet for support.

WHO LAY TO CHUNK

Abundance of words or goods.

WHOLE NEW BALL GAME

Entering into a situation with an entirely different set of rules. Starting from scratch with new maneuvers required.

WHOOP IT UP

Let the good times roll. Party time. Going on a spree.

WHOOPSIE DAISY

Admitting a mistake or error in judgment. Uh-oh!

WHOPPY JAWED

Out of alignment.

WHO PULLED YOUR CHAIN?

Stay out of this conversation—it's none of your business. Relates to the early flushing commode where the flush was activated by a chain and pulley mechanism.

WHOSE SIDE ARE YOU ON, ANYWAY?

A friend's well-intentioned help turns into a deterrent to the successful completion of your project.

WHO'S GUARDING THE STORE?

What are you doing here? Did you leave someone in command when you left?
A person seen in a different place from his regularly assigned station is asked: "...?"

WHO'S HE TRYNG TO KID?

We know a lie when we hear it.

WHO'S ON FIRST?

Relates to a vaudeville routine.
Disorganization, unrelenting confusion and turmoil brings the remark, "...?"

WHO WAS YOUR SLAVE LAST WEEK?

Answer to inappropriate request for help. I will not do what you have asked.

WHY BUY THE COW WHEN MILK IS SO CHEAP?

Don't get married.

WHY DIDN'T I THINK OF THAT?

A new idea you were capable of developing brings the remark, "...?"

WHY DON'T YOU BE LIKE A TREE AND LEAF?

"Leaf" is a pun on "leave." Sardonic humor fitting the case of a pestering younger sibling.

WHY, HE'S SO BRIGHT WE HAVE TO PUT A WASH TUB OVER HIM TO LET THE SUN RISE

Facetiously complimentary, such as when a child brings home a good report card from school.

WHY—I'VE DONE THAT MYSELF

Reassuring a person who has made a mistake.

WHY ME?

After a series of misfortunes a person examines the reasons questioningly.

WHY ON EARTH?

Could you tell me one good reason for your stupid actions.

WHY PUT ANOTHER RAIL ON THE FENCE—THE COWS WILL JUST LEARN TO JUMP ONE HIGHER

An excuse to sell the cattle.

[Rail fences made of split logs were common confinement structures for livestock in the hills in the old days but had their faults.]

WIDE OPEN

Throttle fully advanced to obtain top speed. "I can't go any faster, I've got it ...."

Vulnerable to attack. "Without insurance you are leaving yourself ... for damage claims."

The position of a sports player. "The receiver was ...."

To split. "He split that watermelon ... with one whack of the knife."

Where anything goes. "The mining town with its prostitutes and bars is a ... city."
Plenty of elbow room. "I'm moving out west to the ... spaces."

WIDE SPOT IN THE ROAD
A very small town.

WIDOW'S HUMP
A slumping of the shoulders as a result of extreme dejection, sorrow and old age.

WILD AND WOOLLY AND FULL OF FLEAS AND NEVER BEEN CURRIED ABOVE THE KNEES
Uninhibited, but relates to a virgin female.
Curry: To dress the coat of a horse with a curry comb.

WILD AS FIRE
Uninhibited.

[THE] WILD GOOSE DONE FLEW
Too late. Missed opportunity.

WILD HAIR
Ridiculous idea.

WILD HORSES COULDN'T KEEP ME AWAY
Determined to attend an event.
"Are you going to the wedding?" "...."

WILD MAN
A young male who parties extensively and exuberantly.

WILL IT SADDLE?
Inquiring as to the ability of a horse to carry its rider with one or more of the known smooth riding gaits.
Examples of the gaits: foxtrot, canter and singlefoot.

WILL WONDERS NEVER CEASE?
I'm amazed.
"... You arrived at the meeting on time for a change."

WIND IT UP

Complete a project. Finish the task at hand.
"Are you ready to ...?" "Yes, we're 'bout wound up."
Contrastingly can be said as, "wind it down."

WINK OUT

To die. Usually used in the death of a baby chick.

WIPE THE SLATE CLEAN

Start over. Settle an old debt.

WISE UP PILLS

Said to a person who acts in a way not commensurate with his ability.
Frequently used in reference to oneself.
Someone pulls a boner and you say: "You had better take some ...."

WISH BOOK

Sales catalog.

WISH I HAD MORE ZAP

Lack of energy brings this desire.
Variation: Wish I had more zip.

WISH I HAD THAT AND YOU HAD A BETTER ONE

Admiring one's possessions.

WISH IT WOULD STAY LIKE THIS A WHILE AND THEN GET PRETTY

Wishing for the continuation of an already beautiful day.

WISH ME LUCK

Said by a person departing on a questionable mission.

WITH FRIENDS LIKE THAT, WHO NEEDS ENEMIES?

An injustice is done by a supposed friend.

WITHIN HANDS REACH

Nearby.
"Keep your ammunition ...."

WITHIN SPITTING DISTANCE
Very close.

WITH MY OWN EYES
Will wonders never cease?
"... I saw him open the car door for his wife."

WITHOUT A WHIMPER
Under duress without complaining.

WITHOUT FAIL
I can attest with certainty that it will happen.

WOE IS ME
Self pity.

WOLF IN SHEEP'S CLOTHING
Malicious fake.

WOMEN ARE A NECESSITY ONLY TO THE NEXT GENERATION
Answer to overzealous women's libber.

WOMEN ARE NO DAMN GOOD, GOD BLESS THEM
Can't live with 'em and can't live without 'em.

WONDER WHERE THE SUMMER WAGES WENT
Woke up one morning and snow was on the ground and had no funds.

WON'T AMOUNT TO A HILL OF BEANS
Tempest in a teapot. Much ado about nothing. Of little importance.

WON'T BE NOTHING LEFT BUT A GREASY SPOT
A miscalculation in crossing a busy street on foot could bring this result.

WON'T BE NOTICED ON A GALLOPING HORSE AT MIDNIGHT
Worry not about a small flaw in the clothing.

WON'T TAKE NO FOR AN ANSWER
Persistent.

WON'T TURN LOOSE UNTIL IT THUNDERS OR THE SUN GOES DOWN
Attesting to the tenacity of the bite of a snapping mud turtle.

WON'T WEIGH 90 POUNDS DRIPPING WET
Very slight of build.
Small, skinny, lightweight.

WOOLLY BOOGER
Difficult, strenuous, dangerous task.
Also refers to "hairy" people of questionable character.

WORKING FOR THE MAN
Employed by someone other than self.

WORK RINGS AROUND
A person's estimate of his capacity for labor when compared to another.
"I can ... him."

WORLDS APART
Widely divergent in views or appearance.

WORLDS OF GRASS
Lush pastures.

WORTH ITS WEIGHT IN GOLD
An indispensable tool. A very useful object.

WOULDN'T GIVE YOU A NICKEL FOR A BUSHEL BASKET FULL
Poor quality merchandise.
Something you do not care for.
"... of world series baseball tickets."

WOULDN'T MISS IT FOR THE WORLD
An event of great importance which demands your presence.

WOULDN'T PULL THE HAT OFF YOUR HEAD
Poor running tractor or truck.

WOULDN'T PUT IT PAST HIM
Do not trust this person, he would do anything to achieve his goals, legal or not. A question of audacity.

WOULDN'T TAKE A MILLION DOLLARS FOR ONE OF MY KIDS—BUT I WOULDN'T GIVE YOU A NICKEL FOR ANOTHER ONE
A sardonic expression of the tribulations connected with child rearing.

WOULDN'T TRUST HIM ANY FURTHER THAN I COULD THROW HIM
Totally convinced of one's dishonesty.

WOULD YOU BELIEVE?
Incredible rare occurrence.

WOUND UP
Excited to the point of hysteria.
Also to end a project.

WRAP IT UP
Conclude project.

WRAPPED AROUND HER LITTLE FINGER
Control by playing on the affections of another.
Usually refers to a father-daughter relationship.
"She has him ...."

WRITE WHEN YOU GET WORK
Let us know when you get settled in your new location.

X

X MARKS THE SPOT
The center of where it has or will occur.

Y

YEA, BOY!
Answer to thank you. You're welcome.

YEAH, MAN, I'M WITH YOU
I understand and agree with what you are saying.

YEAR IN, YEAR OUT
Steady and reliable over a long period of time.

YE GODS, WHAT A PIG!
Ugly woman. Wouldn't touch her with a ten-foot pole.

YELLOW STREAK DOWN HIS BACK A MILE WIDE
Very cowardly.
"I called his bluff but he didn't do a thing. I think he has a ...."

YES, MOMMA
Offspring's affectionate or somewhat sardonic answer to a scolding or bit of unsolicited advice from maternal parent.

YOU AIN'T JUST WHISTLING DIXIE
What you say is true.

YOU AIN'T SEEN NOTHING YET
After accomplishment, a new higher one is promised.

YOU ARE NOT GOING—PERIOD!
A request for permission to withdraw to other climes that is

denied with no chance for rebuttal.
Usually a parent-child exchange.

YOU ASKED FOR IT AND YOU'RE GONNA GET IT

Popped off once too often. Invited trouble.

YOU BET

You're welcome. Also, approval of any suggestion.
You say to a customer "much obliged." He answers, "...."
"Are you going to the sale with me tomorrow?" "...."

YOU BETTER BELIEVE IT

Absolutely true regardless of your opinion as to the veracity of the statement.

YOU CAN BANK ON THAT

A guarantee to the nth degree.
I stake my reputation as an honest person on it being true.

YOU CAN BET YOUR BOOTS ON THAT

A sure thing here and you can bet on it.

YOU CAN BET YOUR BOTTOM DOLLAR

A sure thing.

YOU CAN BREATHE

Said after cleaning out a cluttered and overcrowded room.

YOU CAN LEAD A HORSE TO WATER BUT YOU CAN'T MAKE HIM DRINK

Recalcitrant follower is brought to a task by persuasion but then refuses to help with the project.

YOU CAN MAKE MORE MONEY HERE IN THE CITY BY ACCIDENT THAN YOU CAN DOWN ON THE FARM ON PURPOSE

Admonition from city to country cousin.

YOU CAN PICK YOUR FRIENDS BUT NOT YOUR RELATIVES

Skeletons in the closet.
The best of families have some bad apples.

YOU CAN SET YOUR CLOCK BY

Regularly punctual.

YOU CAN TAKE THAT TO THE BANK

A verifiable truth.

YOU CAN'T FIGHT CITY HALL

No use trying to right a wrong in a controversy with a governmental body.

YOU CAN'T GET IT THROUGH YOUR THICK SKULL

Addressing a proven numskull.

YOU CAN'T TAKE IT WITH YOU

Death separates one from material possessions.

YOU COTTON-PICKING CHICKEN-PLUCKER

A belittling insult.
"Get your eyes off my girl, ..."

YOU COULD HAVE HEARD A PIN DROP

Silence after an asinine statement or any surprise announcement.

YOU COULD HAVE KNOCKED ME OVER WITH A FEATHER

So stunned, shocked, and amazed that one is left in a severely weakened condition.
"When my girlfriend told me she was pregnant, ..."

YOU DAMN WELL BETCHA

Emphatic certainty.
"... I'll be there."

YOU'D BETTER WATCH YOUR STEP

A stern warning.

The path you are taking will lead to trouble if you don't change your ways.

YOU DIG YOUR GRAVE WITH A FORK AND A SPOON

You are what you eat. The quantity and quality of the food consumed in large part determines health and longevity.

YOU DONE GOOD

Complimentary remark at the conclusion of a successful mission.

YOU DON'T COUNT

A person of little importance at the moment, or has no vote in a particular decision.

YOU DON'T HAVE TO BE CRAZY TO BE A FARMER, BUT IT HELPS

A sane person would probably not choose such a challenging occupation.

YOU DON'T WANT THAT; IT WILL JUST WEAR A HOLE IN YOUR POCKET

Picking up someone else's dropped coin.

YOU GET WHAT YOU PAY FOR

Competing with quality rather than price. Cheap merchandise is not always the best buy.

YOU GOT A BEE IN YOUR BONNET?

Agitated, excited, overly disturbed by a minor irritation.

YOU GOT A PATENT ON THAT?

A piece of equipment in need of repair.
As you close a rickety, patched-up gate, a neighbor remarks, "...?"

YOU GOT TOOK

Cheated on a deal.
"If you paid over two dollars for it ...."

YOU GOT YOUR WORK CUT OUT FOR YOU

A very difficult task ahead that you are committed to complete.

YOU GREW UP WIPING YOUR NOSE ON YOUR SLEEVE JUST LIKE THE REST OF US

Said to one of common background who has become famous and starts putting on airs. A putdown to the arrogant.
Similar to: "We all put our pants on one leg at a time."

YOU HAVEN'T GOT A PRAYER OF A CHANCE

Success highly doubtful in my opinion.

YOU HAVEN'T MISSED A THING

Nothing happened or was worth seeing.

YOU HAVEN'T PAID THE PREACHER OR BEATEN YOUR WIFE LATELY

Reason for a neighbor getting a needed rain shower on his farm and you didn't.

YOU INSECT

I care not for your company.
Expression of a low opinion.

YOU JUMP ON HIM EVERY TIME HE TURNS AROUND

Constant heckling.

YOU KNOW HOW THAT GOES

Familiar with the same problems.

YOU'LL GET THE POISON

Admonition to not come in contact with a poison ivy vine.

YOU'LL JUST HAVE TO SUFFER

Living under adverse circumstances with little likelihood of improvement.

YOU'LL LIVE
Said to a hypochondriac or anybody complaining.

YOU'LL MAKE IT
Encouragement to a dejected individual after a series of misfortunes.

YOU LOOK LIKE AN ORPHAN
Mother to her beragged child.

YOU LOOK LIKE DEATH WARMED OVER
Usually used in reference to the appearance of a person suffering from the effects of overindulgence in alcohol the night before.

YOU LOOK LIKE YOU COMBED YOUR HAIR WITH AN EGG BEATER
Disheveled. Uncoiffured.
Answer: "When my hair gets long enough to comb, I will cut it."

YOU LOST OR DO YOU LIVE AROUND HERE?
Said to a neighbor you haven't seen in quite a while.

YOU MAY GET MORE THAN YOU BARGAINED FOR
Picking a fight with a superior opponent, which at the time you think is inferior.
Kitty chasing a honey bee.

YOU MIGHT KNOW
Rain forecast for the day harvest is to start. Just my luck.

YOU MISSED YOUR CALLING
Talent in areas other than the field of endeavor.

YOU NEVER KNOW
What appears obvious may not be as it seems.

YOUNG AT HEART
Youthful outlook on life regardless of age.

YOUNG MAN'S GAME

An activity requiring great amounts of physical and mental resources. Activities which exclude the old.
Making your living as a long haul semi-tractor trailer operator is a ....

YOU OLD STOGIE

Older person set in his ways.
Said sardonically to a younger person who will not go out and party with you.
Literally: a stogie is a cigar.

YOU OUGHTA BE ON THE STAGE—ONE LEAVES IN TEN MINUTES

"A rose turns into a thorn."
Deflation of one's ego.
Refers literally to a stagecoach.

YOU RANG?

What did you say?
Speak up, I didn't understand.

YOUR BREAKFAST IS ON THE OTHER END

Said by a father to his son as he points to rabbit tracks in the snow on a cold winter morning or at the beginning of any assigned task.

YOU'RE A DANDY SPECIMEN

Refers to a barnyard animal or fowl in sorry condition.
A person with a hangover.
Ill-kempt and shabby in appearance.

As you try to sell a group of chickens, a sick one stands out in front of the rest and prospective buyer says, "...."

YOU'RE A GOOD EGG

A person of good personality and sense of humor.
I am proud to be your friend and it is a pleasure to be around you.

YOU'RE ALL WET
I disagree wholeheartedly with you.

YOU'RE A MAN AFTER MY OWN HEART
A friend brings a cool drink to you as you work out in the hot fields far from home. Thanks to a friend for a favor.

YOU'RE DURN (DARN) TOOTIN'
I agree with what you say.

YOU'RE GETTING LAZY IN YOUR OLD AGE
Said to a person of any age who takes up habits of easy living as a result of an unwarranted acquisition of money. Catching a normally early riser in bed late in the morning.

YOU'RE GETTING SMARTER IN YOUR OLD AGE
Usually said to oneself after taking some wise-up pills.

YOU'RE LOOKING AT WHAT'S LEFT OF HIM
Answer to a query of someone's presence. The respondent, in his opinion, has been through some rough times in the past.
"Sir, where would I find the proprietor?" "...."

YOU'RE MORE TROUBLE THAN YOU'RE WORTH
Animal constantly getting out of its enclosure.
Antagonistic associate.

YOU'RE OUT OF LUCK
Scraping the bottom of the pot when you arrive for dinner.
When anything is out of stock or used up.

YOU'RE OUT OF YOUR GOURD
What you say is nonsense.

YOUR EYES LOOK LIKE TWO BURNT HOLES IN A BLANKET
Result of overindulgence in alcoholic beverages or a long period of sleeplessness.

YOUR GOOSE IS COOKED

Get out of my hair.
In deep trouble. Caught in the act.
Doing 75 mph in a 55 mph zone and there sits a patrolman with a radar gun on you.

YOUR HANDS SORE?

Pants unbuttoned or unzipped.
Variation: Your fingers sore?

YOUR LOSS IS OUR GAIN

A well-liked teacher moving from one district to another, or any person moving to a different organization.

YOUR MOUTH DOESN'T RUN ON SHUTTERS, IT RUNS ON BISCUIT CUTTERS

Shut up and eat; you talk too much.

YOUR NAME IS MUD

Said to someone arriving late for work
In deep trouble.

YOUR TIME HAS COME

Preparing for chicken dressing and hog butchering.

YOU SHOULD TALK

Pot calling the kettle black.
One's behavior is as bad as the one being criticized.

YOU SMELL LIKE A TOBACCO SACK

Said to one with smoker's breath.

YOU SURE DO KNOW HOW TO HURT A GUY (FELLOW)

Reaction to a slight.

YOU UP FOR ALL DAY?

Greeting to a person arising late in the day.

YOU'VE GOT A GOLD MINE THERE

Profitable business, or valuable piece of real estate.

YOU'VE GOT IT ALL TO YOURSELF NOW
Leaving a person or animal alone to proceed with the task unaided. Such as leaving a sow in the middle of the night to finish parturition on her own.

YOU'VE GOT IT IN YOUR HOT LITTLE HAND
After payment of a debt.
Possessive location of an object.

YOU'VE GOT TO TOOT YOUR OWN HORN
Calling attention to your strong points is sometimes necessary to achieve success in a venture.

YOU'VE WOOLLIED THAT AROUND SOMETHING AWFUL
Brought to tatters, as a cat mauling a mouse. Also, any idea or suggestion can be woollied over.

YOU WON'T HAVE TO WORRY HOW COLD IT'S GOING TO BE THIS WINTER
Said to a dead chicken just ran over by a truck.

YOU WOULD MAKE A BETTER DOOR THAN A WINDOW
Someone obstructing view.

YOU WOULD MAKE A BETTER WINDOW THAN A DOOR
Move, you are in my way.

YOU YELLOW-BELLIED SAPSUCKER
I have called you a coward and now what are you going to do about it?

Index

D

AFTERWORD

Dear Reader

It is my sincere hope that this book has been as helpful and entertaining as you expected. It was intended to inform and entertain the reader and maybe add a little humor to the mix. A lifetime of remembering and 18 years of collecting and writing have not been in vain if you enjoyed the results.

A second volume of Echoes is now underway. If you would like to contribute sayings and their meanings similar in nature to the preceding pages, feel free to submit to the publisher at the address listed below. Individual credit for the sayings cannot be given.

Thank you!

Roland L. Netzer

Echo Publishing Company
P.O. Box 14482
Springfield, MO 65814-0482, USA

About the Author

Roland Netzer spent his boyhood years on a farm in the Ozark Mountains near Springfield, Missouri. After high school, he completed a tour of duty in aerial photography and photo reconnaissance in the Korean combat zone with the U.S. Navy Air Command. Then Mr. Netzer returned to his beloved Ozark Mountains where he married his wife Kathryn (Katy), raised seven children, and earned a BS in Agriculture Education at Southwest Missouri State and a MS in Agriculture Extension from Missouri University. He pursued a career in agriculture as a Missouri University Agricultural Extension agent, a farm manager, and self-employed organic farmer. Mr. Netzer and his wife, Katy, own and operate farms in Missouri that produce organically grown beef and vegetables.

Currently, Mr. Netzer hosts a weekly television show, KY3 Gardener (NBC affiliate filmed in the Ozarks) that teaches organic farming, gardening and local lore, is President of the Greater Springfield Farmers Market, and enjoys his lifelong love of riding his Harley Davidson motorcycle, fishing, hiking, photography and nature study.

Echo Publishing Co.

To order additional copies of Echoes From the Hills, Volume 1, check your local bookstore or order them directly from Echo Publishing Co.

ORDER BY MAIL CONTINENTAL U.S.

Send the full price of your order (Missouri residents add 6.475% sales tax) in U.S. funds, plus $5.00 postage & handling for each book to:

Echo Publishing Co.
P.O. Box 14482
Springfield, MO 65814-0482, U.S.A.
Web site: www.echopublishingco.com
E-mail address: echopublsh@aol.com

PRICES

- Case Bound (Hard Cover) $19.95
- Perfect Bound (Soft Cover) $14.95

POSTAGE & HANDLING

Outside continental U.S. and international orders:

Airmail–add freight equal to price of each book to total price of order.

NOTE: Orders shipped to Canada and Mexico are sent surface mail at a shipping rate of $5.00 per book.

All books guaranteed or your money back.
Thank You!

Allow 4–6 weeks for delivery on all orders.
Books, postage and handling rates are subject to change.